THE ESSENTIAL GUIDE TO
AIRSOFT GEAR

IN ASSOCIATION WITH

AIRSOFT
INTERNATIONAL

OSPREY
PUBLISHING

OSPREY PUBLISHING

Bloomsbury Publishing Plc

Kemp House, Chawley Park, Cumnor Hill,

Oxford OX2 9PH, UK

1385 Broadway, 5th Floor, New York, NY 10018, USA

E-mail: info@ospreypublishing.com

www.ospreypublishing.com

OSPREY is a trademark of Osprey Publishing Ltd

First published in Great Britain in 2021

© Osprey Publishing Ltd, 2021

A catalogue record for this book is available from the British Library.

ISBN: HB 9781472846396

eBook 9781472846372

ePDF 9781472846389

XML 9781472846365

FSC
www.fsc.org

MIX
Paper from responsible sources
FSC® C016779

21 22 23 24. 25   10 9 8 7 6 5 4 3 2 1

Originated by PDQ Digital Media Solutions, Bungay, UK

Printed and bound in India by Replika Press Private Ltd.

Unless otherwise indicated, all the images in this book are © *Airsoft International Magazine*.

Osprey Publishing supports the Woodland Trust, the UK's leading woodland conservation charity.

To find out more about our authors and books visit **www.ospreypublishing.com**. Here you will find extracts, author interviews, details of forthcoming events and the option to sign up for our newsletter.

CONTENTS

WHAT IS AIRSOFT?

Put your hand up if you ever played "Cowboys and Indians" or "Cops and Robbers" when you were a kid. Yes of course you did. You might not like to admit it to your mates today, but I bet you had a great time.

Airsoft skirmishing is a grown-up version of those simple children's games – that twig you found on the forest floor that you brandished as your rifle has been replaced with state-of-the-art electric or even gas-powered rifles and pistols. That enthusiasm you once had as a child as you stormed your friends' fortified bunker will come rushing back to you as you step onto an Airsoft skirmish field. The kit might be a bit more advanced, and you might be a bit older, but the concept is basically the same.

The concept of skirmishing is quite simple: two opposing teams are set a task to achieve. That task might be as simple as catching the opponents' flag or a more complex task such as finding and securing a downed pilot and escorting him or her back to the safety of your base whilst fending off the opposing team who are intend on recapturing their prisoner.

So how do you know you've been hit? With paintball it is very easy as a splat of paint marks the spot. Airsoft is completely different as the hits are not visible. The games are heavily marshalled, but they are there really to keep a watching brief and ensure player safety. It's all about the player's own sense of honour, knowing when you have been hit and calling yourself out, and either call for a medic or walk back to a designated position to respawn so you can join the game again.

You don't have to be mega fit or cash rich to play as the majority of skirmish sites will hire you all the gear you need to fully immerse yourself into the fantasy world of Airsoft. Once you take the plunge there's no turning back. It won't be long before you find yourself buying your own equipment and becoming a regular at your local skirmish site.

This book is designed to help you look the part on the skirmish field and has pulled together the very best in loadouts from the vast back catalogue of *Airsoft International* magazine.

We will help you identify the clothing and equipment you'll need, whilst keeping an eye on the cost as some equipment has become collectible over the years and comes with a hefty price tag, which quite simply can't be justified for the skirmish field. But with a bit of creativity we will show you how you can either find replica gear at a fraction of the price, or even in some cases talk you through alterations to new gear that can be used as passable alternatives to those hard-to-find costly essentials.

We should at this point mention the safety aspect of skirmishing. One of the main safety issues at all sites is eye protection. Whether it be full-face protection or a cool pair of ballistic-rated eyewear, some form of approved eyewear must be worn. At no point should you ever consider sacrificing your eye protection over your loadout. Smart players will take advantage of a combination of eye protection and face masks, which gives you more freedom than a one-piece full face mask but the same level of protection.

You might become what is affectionately known as a "geardo". You'll see them strutting their stuff in the safe zone comparing their kit and showing off their latest purchase. You might also want to get your company involved. Airsoft is a great training tool for leadership development and team building, or you might just want to become a common or garden player.

Whatever path you take, jump on board and enjoy the ride.

Paul Monaf,
Editor *Airsoft International*

GET STARTED IN AIRSOFT!

Pictures **Paul Monaf**
Featuring **Victoria Trafford**

It's amazing, exciting, action-packed and thrilling, but getting into Airsoft can be a daunting task. There's a lot of questions you need to ask and there's also a lot of mixed opinions on what is essential, what's advisable and what is not worth the hassle.

Airsoft International is laying down a definitive guide on what you need to get started in Airsoft and what to expect when you arrive at your first game. We've no doubt you'll be hooked right away, so we'll also be giving you some advice on what we think are some sound investments to get your show on the road!

For the most part, Airsoft players are a helpful bunch. There will be countless individuals willing to offer up their opinions on what they think you should do to get into Airsoft but the truth is, once you've been in the deep end for even a short while, it's really easy to lose sight of the very beginning. It's a real challenge to think back to the start and what it was like as a new player. You can often find stuff going way over your head as more experienced players reel off jargon and acronyms without even pausing to let you ask what it all means. Fear not, we'll explain it from the very beginning here!

DOES THE GEAR MAKE THE GAME?

If you speak to any reasonably experienced Airsoft player or collector, 99 per cent of the time they will comment on how wallet-squeezingly addictive Airsoft can get and it can be an off-putting factor for many players, but it need not be an expensive hobby to take up and you CAN play Airsoft on a budget.

Head down to your local site and you'll see a variety of stereotypes. There will be guys that are kitted up to the eyeballs, dripping with matching camo, helmets, beeping radio systems and guns with lights, laser, sights and grips bolted all over the place. At the other end of the spectrum, you'll probably spot a few far more casual guys wearing jeans and a hoodie, maybe some will have a lightweight vest or some pouches on a belt but other than that, they will look pretty low-profile and casual.

The principle of Airsoft play is simple though. If even a single BB hits you, you call hit and you are "dead". Depending on the rules of the game you are playing, that might mean that you head back to a respawn and wait five minutes, maybe you go back to a flag and get stuck back in straight away, or maybe you have to call "medic!" until a teammate can assist you. In that sense, it doesn't matter how much gear, pouches, body armour or lasers you have, you are vulnerable to enemy fire just as much as the next man. Of course, there's a contentious issue around whether wearing pouches upon pouches and an armour vest designed to stop AK rounds in real life effects a player's ability to "feel" their hits, but that's something for another time. What you need to play Airsoft is far simpler and you should never feel intimidated or made to feel inferior based on your selection of equipment.

"Most Airsofters will agree, despite the kit and the fancy accessories, some of the most fun they have ever had playing a game was with a simple spring shotgun or a pistol, chasing each other around. That's the basic appeal of Airsoft. It's pure and uncomplicated."

What Do I Need to Play Airsoft?

So what exactly do you need to take part in a game? There are a few essentials that you shouldn't be without. The first and most essential item is eye protection. Everything else, even your gun, pales in comparison to the importance of eye protection.

Eye Pro

Airsoft guns are relatively harmless and even from point-blank range, one within the power limits of the UK will leave you with nothing more than a trivial injury. This is true for your entire body except for two points, your eyes.

At just one joule (328fps on a 0.2g BB) an Airsoft gun discharges a round with enough energy to pop your eyeball like a juicy cherry tomato. If that happens, it's game over. Your eye will not heal, and you will be blinded for good. Given that you only have two eyes, this is something you MUST avoid, and it is easily done. Ballistic goggles and glasses do the job and provided they meet or exceed the relevant standard (in Europe this in EN166), they will be as good as impenetrable. Many players like to use mesh goggles and although these do not have any ballistic standards ratings, practical use has found them to be adequate in terms of protection from injury. Mesh has the benefit of not steaming up or misting like many polycarbonate lenses can, however, the downside is that they can let small particles through that can irritate the eyes, if not cause an injury. Our advice is to use a full-seal goggle that sits directly against your face or even better, a full facemask that protects your teeth too, for your first few games. This will allow you to make your own decision based on personal experience.

Footwear

Almost as essential as eye protection is a good pair of suitable boots. Although you might not suffer life-changing damage from rolling your ankle, it's something you want to avoid, especially if it would prevent you from working, etc. As such, an area we advise new players to invest in as much as they can is the footwear department. You don't have to spend a fortune but what you need to look for is some well-fitting, sturdy boots that are grippy and give you good ankle support. Many Airsoft sites are in thick woodland or dilapidated areas with uneven ground. Since you'll usually be preoccupied with avoiding enemies, BBs or shooting back your own, it's inevitable that the odd trip or stumble will occur, so you need something that instils a little confidence. Some brands to look for are Viper Tactical and Magnum. These companies both make solid, dependable boots that don't cost the earth.

Clothing

Unlike paintball, you won't get covered in oily slime when playing Airsoft but you will probably rip or tear a few pairs of trousers before your first year of gaming is through. Because of this you probably don't want to wear your best jeans and a fancy shirt, although lots of players do like to indulge by buying high-end combat uniforms in matching camouflage patterns. We wouldn't advise doing this straight away unless you have a particular interest in collecting this sort of stuff.

Camouflage is an interesting point in itself and some players will swear that you need to match your surroundings for a competitive edge. In truth, we've found that when used correctly, camouflage can be useful, but we've also seen that it's useless if you don't make the most of it because the ranges you'll find yourself fighting over at an Airsoft game are far shorter than that of "real" combat. You might want to avoid wearing bright red or blue football shirts, but provided you are wearing something dark toned or drab, you won't be at a major disadvantage.

Jeans do make an occasional appearance on an Airsoft site, but it's difficult to recommend them based on the variability of UK weather… If you've ever been caught in a sudden downpour while wearing jeans, you know they get heavy and uncomfortable and also take a long time to dry. Avoid chafing your bits and pieces to shreds and wear something a little lighter. A pair of generic "combat trousers" is a great idea and with the extra cargo pockets, you get a little extra storage space for things like a snack or some spare ammo.

When it's cold, a sweater, hoodie or smock is a favourite item to wear for lots of players but generally, with all the running around you'll be doing, in all but the coldest months, you might find yourself overheating. A simple long-sleeved top or base layer is a great choice.

Vest and Pouches

Although it is possible to play Airsoft with just your gun and a spare magazine or BBs in your pocket, as you get more involved, you are likely to want to invest in some form of load carrying equipment. This will allow you to carry some of the more involved stuff like grenades, a radio, something to drink and maybe a multitool, torch or other accessories.

You'll probably hear the acronym "MOLLE" before long and that refers to a modular manner of attaching pouches to a platform, like a belt, a vest or a chest rig. While it's something you might want to look at in the future, a MOLLE system is quite expensive compared to an alternative. You can configure it however you want but you'll need to invest in a base platform, then each individual pouch, so the cost adds up. The other option is to pick up a fixed configuration vest.

There are loads to choose from and they can be bought at various Airsoft shops or online retailers – the choice is yours. Most have a large space on the back to fit a hydration

carrier and below that, there's normally a small compartment you can use as a utility space, perhaps for stuff you don't need to access quickly. On each side there's space for large pouches that can accept bigger items like a military waterbottle or canteen; even things like a mess tin will fit in there. The front is usually covered in smaller ammo and general-purpose pouches so you can carry magazines and accessories and some even have an internal pocket that you can stow a pistol or small sidearm in. All ammo pouches are normally well sized and will accept magazines for a variety of weapons from the M4, the AK all the way to the MP5 pictured here.

Also when buying think of the sizing, if you are a small person or larger than average size then generic sizes may not be right for you so you may need to go and try a few on for size. After all, comfort is vital.

What Happens at an Airsoft Game?

It sounds like the answer is obvious, but you will undoubtedly ask yourself "what's going to happen when I get to the game?" At some point, there will obviously be shooting, or "skirmishing" as it often gets called, but you don't all just jump out of the car straight away and start hammering BBs at each other.

Most sites open the gates a good couple of hours prior to games actually starting and in that period there will be plenty of time for you to grab a drink, get yourself and your weapon ready and listen to the briefing. In all the years we've been playing, we've encountered lots of briefs, some concise and very to the point, others, well, not so brief. Although it's not the most exciting part of the day, listening

to the briefing is very, very important. You'll be notified of the rules of the site and things you can and cannot do. These might be simple guides to make the games better, but they will also be for your safety and that of other players.

One thing briefings are not is an ear-bashing from some drill sergeant wannabe, at least not at a decent site. As long as everyone pays the staff charged with the responsibility of going through the speech the courtesy of listening, there's no reason for any raised voices.

> "One of the biggest irritations for me, when I'm trying to get a game started, is people talking when they should be listening. Please just leave the chat until after the briefing is done!"
>
> Ross, Head Marshal

Depending on the structure of how the site operates, you might have a briefing before your final kit prep or afterwards but if you have your head screwed on you shouldn't need much more than about 10 minutes to sort yourself out ready to go. All you really want to be looking to getting sorted out at this point in time is filling up your magazines with BBs, tightening up your boots and making sure your gun's battery is connected.

Now isn't the time to start trying to perform modifications to your guns and the parcel shelf of your car isn't a good spot for rebuilding your gun, it never ends well and you'll more than likely lose some miniscule but essential screw or component. Once you are ready to go, you'll more than

likely be ushered to take part in a procedure called "chronographing".

Chrono'ing, as it's generally known, isn't an invasive procedure, it's merely ensuring your gun is within the power levels allowed at that site. Most sites in the UK operate a 345fps upper limit on guns that are capable of full auto. Most guns purchased in the UK will be sold well under that limit and will be useable.

If your gun is over the limit, you'll be asked to not use it until it has been reduced in power. You won't find yourself in trouble, as these things happen, and it's been found out at the beginning of the day, but you might if you knowingly enter the gaming area with a gun you don't know the power of. If in doubt, check beforehand and if that's not possible, prepare for the worst by securing the use of a spare gun. Once everyone is chrono'd some sites will tag guns that have passed with a coloured zip tie or sticker. Now the real fun starts!

Most sites will run games with two or more "teams"… The players will generally be split up between the various teams, and if you have travelled along with friends or a group, that group will generally be allowed to stick together. You'll make your way to the start points for your respective teams and at that point, one of the marshals will run you through the game scenario. At this point continue to listen attentively. You'll have a better and more successful day if you keep track of what objectives you are set to complete and you'll also ensure you are at the centre of the action. Finally, you'll get the sounding of "game on" and it's time to get on the trigger!

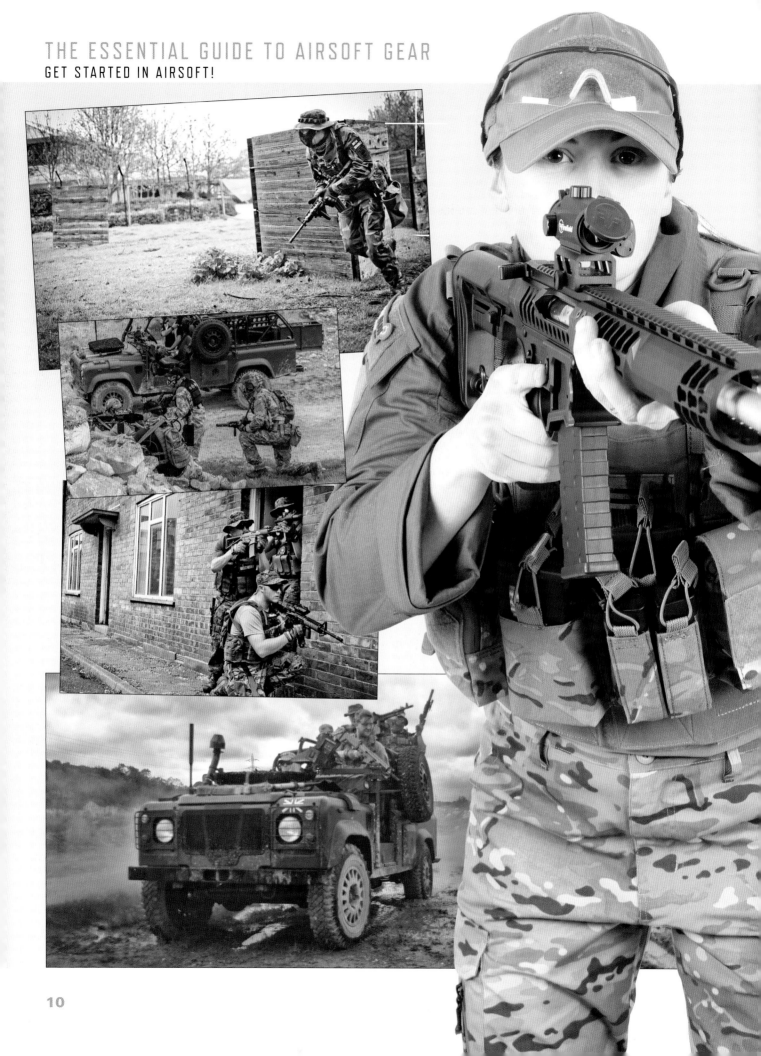

BUYING IN!

There are many brands out there that are ideal for the novice and less experienced player.

Viper Tactical, Taiwan Gun and Invader Gear are our go-to brands for affordable and reliable kit that won't let you down.

- Invader Gear Combat Shirt
- 8Fields Buckle Up Chest Rig
- 8Fields Low Pro Body Armour
- EmersonGear Jogger Pants
- 8Fields Knee Pads

Our model is also wearing some additional and optional extras including some protective tactical gloves and a neck scarf, which is useful for adding some protection around the face and neck. You may wish to consider these extras when you get started in Airsoft.

→ 8Fields
Low Pro Body
Armour

CHAPTER ONE

US ODA SCUD HUNTERS

Featuring **James Goulding**
with special thanks to **Marcus Stacey-Bradbury**

During the 1991 Gulf War, in response to coalition airstrikes against Saddam Hussein's forces a series of SCUD missiles were launched at the heart of Israel. Whist these missiles were outdated and inaccurate, the threat was real and had a huge political impact. So, it's not surprising that a coalition air and ground task force was formed to go "SCUD Hunting".

Coalition commanders deployed Special Operations Forces on the ground, which saw US ODA or Delta Force teams along with British SAS operators. Their mission was simple – to seek out and destroy SCUDs, their launchers and the infrastructure that supported them.

READY ROOM

US Army Delta was assigned an area of desert to the north-west of the Iraqi city of Al Qaim, which was known as SCUD boulevard. Once on the ground in Iraq, their job was to call in Coalition airstrikes against SCUD locations. Once the war was over military analysts began to question whether coalition Special Forces had destroyed any actual SCUDs, or instead had targeted decoys that the Iraqis were believed to have deployed. Whatever the material impact of their operations, the clothing and gear the ODA teams used is very much a unique loadout that has to be recreated.

LOAD BEARING GEAR

The US Military Enhanced Tactical Load Bearing Vest was an integral part of the Individual Integrated Fighting System (IIFS). The IIFS was deployed in 1988, to serve as a fighting carrying system and was seen as a replacement for the dated All-Purpose Lightweight Individual Carrying Equipment (ALICE). The concept of a load-carrying vest is that the weight of the equipment carried is more evenly distributed over the body. The vest has integrated pockets that can hold six mags and two grenades. The vest can also be augmented with ALICE ammo, utility and water pouches.

This tactical vest, albeit a replica, is the enhanced version which is considered to be the second generation of the original design. This enhanced vest features mesh backing which provides better cooling and is fully adjustable, giving you the ability to wear your combat gear tightly to your body.

The original design and trial version of the Tactical Load Bearing Vest incorporated panels made of Kevlar, to improve personal protection, when worn in conjunction with the Personnel Armour System for Ground Troops (PASGT) flak vest. But the concept was soon canned as the Kevlar added unnecessary weight.

Along with what was at the time a new and exciting tactical load carrying vest, a new individual equipment belt was also introduced, featuring a black plastic ITW Fastex quick-release buckle and redesigned adjustment system. It was decided that instead of contracting new individual ALICE components in the Woodland camouflage pattern, the remainder of the already existing and widely available ALICE components would be utilised with the IIFS. These were mainly the water canteen cover, field first aid dressing case, entrenching tool cover and small arms ammunition cases.

← Water bottle

The IIFS fighting load consists of the following standard issue components:

- Belt, Individual Equipment
- Vest, Ammunition Carrying
- Vest, Tactical Load Bearing
- ALICE system components
- Carrier, Entrenching Tool
- Case, Field First Aid Dressing
- Cover, Water Canteen
- Magazine pouch

↑ ALICE pouch

Features:

This Mil-Tec replica copies the real world version in every aspect, but is less expensive than a real version that you will find in numerous army surplus outlets.

- One size fits most
- Four fixed M4/M16 magazine pouches
- Two fixed grenade pockets
- Adjustable padded shoulders
- Adjustable waist
- Nylon straps for tactical belt
- D-rings
- Outer fabric: 600D nylon, polyurethane coated
- Strong mesh body
- EVA foam padding in shoulders

Available from Military 1st
www.military1st.co.uk

→ M81 Mil-Tec Load Bearing Vest

→ POLARTEC WATCH CAP

It's a simple black fleece military cap, in fact, a Polartec 300 beanie, that's still used by American forces today, which to be fair is nothing out of the ordinary and quite a mundane piece of gear to have in your locker.

Polartec have a long history that dates back well over 100 years. In 1981 the company created a synthetic fabric technology that was more lightweight, breathable, and faster drying than all its predecessors. Polartec fleece established itself as the benchmark for insulating materials and forever changed the way the world dresses for cold weather. This invigorated the entire outdoor industry and cemented the company's roots as pioneers of innovation. Their fleece remains a premier insulating fabric with versatile capabilities and an ever-growing list of applications so you can see why the

military was quick to jump on the Polartec bandwagon. In fact, the Watch Cap was part of the Gen II Extended Cold Weather Clothing System (ECWCS), which also featured a Polartec 300 jacket (amongst other layers) that would have certainly been used during the bitterly cold nights in the Iraq desert.

LONG CUFF PILOT GLOVES

The gloves are pretty simple for this project and true to the timeline. Nomex pilot gloves were at the time a firm favourite with Special Forces types as they were pretty much the only piece of clothing that they used that had any protection from fire.

"Nomex" is a flame-resistant, meta-aramid material developed in the 1960s and quickly adopted by a number of industries. Aramid is closely related to nylon but has strong and heat-resistant synthetic fibres. The military first adopted the material for pilot gloves, and later flying suits, and the gloves have been eagerly adopted by the Special Forces community, who to this day still use Nomex pilot gloves due not only to their protection, but also their suppleness and fit.

CLOTHING

Here you can really go to town with camo patterns that are very much in the minority and hardly ever seen on skirmish fields, but what great combinations! Desert Night Camouflage was designed in 1976. Its purpose was to conceal soldiers from the older generation of enemy night vision devices (NVDs). The pattern is now considered obsolete by the US military, but still very much in demand with collectors and the Airsoft community. The camouflage really came into its own during the Gulf War, when US troops were issued with over-jackets (with a removable insulating liner) and over-trousers, both being designed to be worn over the issued six-colour Desert Battle Dress Uniform (DBDU). US Desert Night Camouflage – albeit obsolete – remains to this day the only Desert Night Camo to be issued to US troops. However, the pattern does occasionally pop up on US Special Forces types and has become a very popular camouflage within the collector and Airsoft communities and is very well worth looking into for its uniqueness.

The DBDU itself is a US arid-environment camouflage battle uniform first issued in the early 1980s, but which came into its own during the First Gulf War. Despite the US military moving on, a testament to the effectiveness of this unique six-colour camouflage is that it is still in use to this day by many countries' military forces.

Designed back in the early 1960s when the US Army believed that it might need to intervene in the Arab–Israeli

conflicts, the six-pattern camouflage quickly became known as "chocolate-chip camouflage" or "cookie dough camouflage" due to it resembling chocolate-chip cookie dough. The uniform's pattern is constructed around a light tan base overlaid with broad swathes of pale green and wide two-tone bands of brown. Clusters of black and white spots are scattered over the camouflage to mimic the appearance of pebbles and their shadows.

Chocolate-Chip Camouflage uniforms were not issued in any number until the 1980s when it became the US Army's first fully functional desert combat pattern and remained so until 1992. However, during its 12-year service reports suggested that the design contrasted too much with the terrain, preventing the camouflage from blending in effectively. Anecdotal evidence suggested that the dark areas of the pattern warmed up more than the paler parts under desert sunlight, and retained the heat longer. The six colours were also more expensive to manufacture than three or four colours, and the need for a camouflage that would be suitable for use in any desert resulted in a requirement for a new desert camouflage uniform. The US Army Natick System Center began the search for a substitute.

PROPPER UNIFORM BDU TROUSERS, SIX-COLOUR DESERT

- Durable zip fly with button
- Two large hand pockets
- Two back pockets with buttoned flaps
- Two expandable side cargo pockets with buttoned flaps and side drainage
- Fused flaps for neat look
- Reinforced seat and knees for added durability and protection
- Side waist adjusters for perfect fit
- Seven belt loops
- Adjustable drawstring leg closures
- Felled inseams, outseams and seat seams for added comfort
- Fade-, shrink- and wrinkle-resistant polycotton ripstop fabric
- Material: 60 per cent cotton, 40 per cent polyester

Available from Military 1st
www.military1st.co.uk

↓ BDU Trousers
Six-Colour Desert

↘ **Desert Classic Shemagh**

CHAPTER TWO

BRAVO TWO ZERO

Featuring **James Goulding**

Bravo Two Zero was the callsign of a British Army Special Air Service (SAS) patrol on the ground in Iraq during the First Gulf War. Dependant on whose account you believe, the eight-man patrol was either given the task of gathering intelligence (Chris Ryan's account) or destroying Iraqi SCUD missile launchers (Andy McNab's account). The patrol has been the subject of several books and a film over the years, all with very conflicting stories on what might or might not have happened, leading to some questioning whether the patrol ever actually existed?

Former SAS soldier Michael Asher traced in person the route of the patrol and interviewed local Iraqi witnesses; he reported that two of the books written by patrol members – McNab's *Bravo Two Zero* and Ryan's *The One That Got Away* – were largely fabrications. His findings were published in a documentary filmed by Channel 4 Television and in a 2002 book entitled *The Real Bravo Two Zero*.

READY ROOM

According to well-documented reports, each member of the patrol wore desert DPM with a World War II-era sand-coloured desert smock and regular issue army boots.

Although the vast majority of kit they used is readily available through many online stores, some pieces of kit you will have to be creative with, not because of their price, but their availability. However, Ryan, the one member of the patrol who was never captured and who claimed to have made SAS history with the longest escape and evasion as he made his way to Syria, covering 180 miles (290km) on foot, wore a pair of £100 "brown Raichle Gore-Tex-lined hiking boots." Each member carried a belt kit, and some wore 72 Pattern assault vests, a Bergen rucksack, one sandbag of food, one sandbag containing two NBC suits, extra ammunition bandoliers and a 5 imp gal (23l) jerry can of water. The belt kit included ammunition, water, food and trauma-care equipment. The rucksack contained 25 kilos of sandbags and observation post equipment, seven days' worth of rations, spare batteries for the radio, demolition equipment (including PE4 plastic explosive, detonators, and both Claymore and Elsie anti-personnel mines) and further medical supplies.

← WORLD WAR II DESERT SMOCK

A cotton Gabardine windproof garment that was first issued in the 1940s to commando types and the Long Range Desert Group (LRDG). Because of the long service life of this piece of issued clothing, many soldiers would have been issued this smock right up to and including the Bravo Two Zero mission.

The smock itself isn't that expensive, but more of an ultra-rare item, which is surprising considering the number of smocks that were produced over the years. You can expect to spend around £250, and for a good condition, dated example well over £1,000! The repro version we have used is priced around £100 and was initially supplied by Soldier of Fortune, but this is becoming a bit of a collector's item in its own right.

Thankfully there is an alternative repro version available, much heavier than the original and Soldier of Fortune's version due to its heavy cotton drill manufacture which is also reasonably windproof and will more than do the job.

DESERT DPM

Disruptive Pattern Material (DPM) was first issued to the British Army in 1960. It uses the four basic western European temperate colours of black, dark brown, mid-green and dark sand to make a very effective camouflage that has survived in its basic design, with no more than slight changes to the colours and pattern, until its decommissioning with the British armed forces in favour of Multi-Terrain Pattern (MTP) in 2010. We suspect that DPM was first issued in minimal numbers, until 1966 when the army introduced a camouflage field uniform. Known informally as the 1966 Pattern, this was, in fact, identical in design to the 1960 Pattern kit. Throughout DPM's history, there have been minor changes in design and colour, fast-forwarding some 35 years to the Combat Soldier 95 clothing system, which has similar colours to the 1966 uniform. However, instead of all four colours printed onto a whitish base, the material is woven in the sand shade and overprinted only with three colours.

Initially seen in the 1980s, the first variant of Desert DPM consisted of a mixture of subdued sand and khaki but was quickly replaced by a two-colour light brown on sand version. By 1990 a four-colour (light and dark browns, khaki, and sand) version had been adopted by some Middle Eastern countries, notably Kuwait. Although slight changes have been made to DPM through its long history with the British armed forces, the pattern is easy to recognise and in abundance on the surplus market making the uniform extremely cheap to purchase.

72 PATTERN WEBBING

The 72 (or 75) Pattern Webbing was a new system made out of PU-coated nylon and designed to replace the old 58 Pattern Webbing, but it never got past the trial stages with the British Army.

Originally designed to counter the Soviet NBC capability it was intended to be used in a variety of environments including the desert. The package included ammunition pouches, utility pouches, a backpack and yoke, plus an assault vest that did see operational use by the SAS in Dhofar, the Gulf War and the Falklands.

The assault vest was basic and raw by today's standards. Two large front pockets and a backpack were held together with mesh shoulder straps, side adjustment straps and two front fastening straps. Although not a mega-priced item of kit, it remains a sought-after prize in the collector/re-enactment world, where discontinued replicas can match the price of an authentic original vest. This is where problems arise with the loadout; it's a case of availability versus cost. Both replica and original vests do occasionally come up for sale, but they are very few and far between and can cost upwards of £300 for a replica and vastly more for the real thing.

But being a bit creative here (for the skirmish field) will save you money and stress. The easy option is to ditch the idea of a vest completely and load yourself up with Personal Load Carrying Equipment (PLCE) webbing and an NI Chest Rig, just as the majority of the patrol would have done, but there is a solution for the skirmish field from the US tactical gear giant S.O.Tech.

← 72 Pattern Webbing

← Beanie Hat

↑ Nomex Flight Gloves

S.O.TECH RECCE VEST

Designed as a lightweight vest, the Recce Vest is a modern-day take on the original 72 Pattern Assault Vest. It is an almost identical design to the original vest and features two large front pockets, plus a backpack and mess shoulder straps. The manufacturer recognises that their vest took its inspiration directly from the 72 Pattern Vest, adding on their website,

> "Those original vests have become sought after items. This vest has had some improvements over the U.K. models with flap or shock cord retention on the two smaller front pouches. You can engage the flap, or fold it away to use just the shock cord. We also added a storm hood to the backpack for retention. The vest is made from 500 denier Cordura for lightweight durability."

The one big problem here, apart from the fact that this vest is an imposter, is the vest's colour option. A tin of O.D. and tan Krylon soon remedied this problem. You can, of course, hold out for a real or more authentic replica to come up for sale – the choice is yours. We like to find cost-effective and straightforward alternatives, which in our opinion capture the essence of a 72 Pattern Vest, which is more than adequate for the skirmish field.

Key features:

- Six fully adjustable straps
- Mesh support straps
- Five compartments (four front pockets, one rear pack)
- Dual closure options for smaller front pockets
- Lightweight design
- Elastic strap retention
- Dimensions: rear pack – 10 x 12 x 4.5in
- Large front pockets – 9.5 x 6 x 2.5in
- Smaller front pockets – 5 x 4 x 1.5in
- Material: 500D Cordura Nylon®, elastic, polymer buckles, heavy webbing. Made in the USA

→ **S.O.Tech Recce Vest**

PLCE WEBBING

PLCE or Personal Load Carrying Equipment has been in service from the mid 1980s and exists in three different patterns, 85, 90 and the 95 Pattern. It was designed as a webbing system to improve how a British soldier could operate for 48 hours or conduct a mission-specific task. The basic set-up consists of a belt, a shoulder harness and several pouches.

The PLCE webbing system is produced from double-layered 1000 Denier, which was internally rubberised into a Cordura Nylon, making it a long-lasting and hard-wearing fabric, and creating a fighting belt order that is still in use with the British armed forces today.

The Infantry Trials and Development Unit (ITDU), based in Warminster, conducted trials with the PLCE webbing system. It decided the system was fit for purpose, and divided it into three specific orders of dress:

Assault Order

The Assault Order consists of the very essentials needed to conduct a military task in the theatre of war. Ammunition, the water bottle, the entrenching tool, the bayonet, the helmet, and CBRN (Chemical, Biological, Radiological, and Nuclear) protective clothing (stowed in one of the detachable side pouches of the rucksack) all to be carried in operations and patrols of only short duration.

Combat Order

The Combat Order consists of the Assault Order with the addition of the means of stowage for rations and personal equipment, which enables the British soldier to live and fight for 24 hours. In practice, the patrol packs are used by many units and individual soldiers instead of the side pouches, as they are found to be larger in size and more convenient.

Marching Order

The Marching Order is the Combat Order wiht the addition of the rucksack (Bergen) and is the fighting loadout required for operations of more than two weeks, without means of resupply, except for ammunition, rations and water. The complete Bergen (with side pouches attached) is carried.

→ PLCE Webbing

NI CHEST RIG

Described as "probably one of the most awesome chest rigs ever made" the NI or Northern Ireland Chest Rig was designed to be the multi-tool of chest rigs carrying everything a soldier would need in combat.

A much lighter alternative to the PLCE webbing, it is made of the same top quality Cordura and features as many pouches as this kind of rig can take. There are three magazine pouches designed to carry three 5.56mm mags each, utility pouches on the sides, and a large internal map pocket. It also features a piece of PLCE belt on the backside for additional pouches (ALICE pouches will fit too). The magazine and utility pouches both have a Velcro and Fastex clip for versatility, so technically it's possible to carry AK magazines also (each mag pouch takes in one AK-type magazine). The shoulder and waist straps can be adjusted quite freely and have a lot of movement, meaning that the larger-framed player won't have a problem with the fit.

CHAPTER THREE

BLACK HAWK DOWN

Featuring Dave Porter and Jason Green

Some of the most popular loadout features from our archives cover the US Special Forces operators from Delta Force, and none more so than at the time of Operation *Gothic Serpent*, the operation that provided the raw material for the book and film *Black Hawk Down*.

This disastrous raid against a Somali warlord shattered the confidence of the world's only superpower and had a far-reaching effect on US military policy. We have featured this subject a number of times in the magazine, and this is the most thorough treatment yet. We have tried to raise the bar and take a look at two different styles of Delta from both a Hollywood and a realistic point of view. We have recreated the look and feel of the 75th Ranger Regiment who fought alongside US Army Delta in Somalia.

Operation *Gothic Serpent* took place in Somalia in 1993 and was instigated by the US Joint Special Operations Command (JSOC) which had deployed during the Somali Civil War. Its goal was to capture Mohamed Farrah Aidid, one of the principal Somali warlords. As part of the operation, soldiers were tasked with the arrest of two of Aidid's lieutenants. That mission became known as the Battle of Mogadishu, and that is the episode that was dramatized in the Hollywood blockbuster *Black Hawk Down*.

In December 1992, the US Army joined the ongoing UN operation in Somali called Operation *Restore Hope*. Its mission was to restore law and order in war-torn Somalia, which at the time seemed to be working as some months after the US forces intervened a disarmament conference was proposed by the leading Somali faction leader, Mohamed Farrah Aidid, who had been leader of the political grouping the United Somali Congress and had formed the Somali National Alliance in 1992. The alliance members were leaders of factions who all recognised Aidid's authority, who by this point had declared himself Somalia's president. The UN presence was not welcomed by the alliance, or for that matter by the vast majority of Somali civilians, and this resulted in many of them, including women and children, taking up arms and actively resisting the UN's forces during the civil war in Mogadishu.

One of the deadliest attacks on UN forces saw 24 Pakistani soldiers ambushed and killed in an Aidid-controlled area of Mogadishu on 5 June. After that, it soon became apparent that there was little hope of any peaceful resolution of the situation. Shortly after the murder of the 24 soldiers, an emergency session of the UN Security Council was called, and Resolution 837 was issued, which ordered the arrest and trial of those that carried out the ambush. The US Air Force and UN troops then mounted an unsuccessful raid to capture Aidid, which further escalated the violence between Somalis and UN forces.

↓ Mogadishu, Somalia, 1993: members of the famous B Co, 3/75 Rangers immediately prior to the "Battle of the Black Sea". Visible in the left and right background are MH-6 Little Bird helicopters with folded main rotor blades. (Courtesy 75th Ranger Regiment)

TASK FORCE RANGER

After many attacks on US troops, which saw four Military Police killed and several soldiers wounded, 400 Rangers, Delta operators, SEALS, PJs and Combat Controllers were deployed to Mogadishu with the sole purpose of finding Aidid, which eventually culminated in the Battle of Mogadishu. The mission was simple: seize two of Aidid's high-echelon lieutenants who would be attending a meeting in the city.

← Bravo Company, 3rd Battalion of the 75th Rangers, pictured on the beach adjacent to their hangar in Mogadishu immediately prior to the mission on 3 October 1993. (Courtesy US Army, 75th Ranger Regiment)

Although this was achieved, the situation spiralled rapidly out of control with Ranger PFC Todd Blackburn, from Chalk Four, falling while fast-roping. Blackburn suffered an injury to his head and back of his neck and was evacuated by SGT Jeff Struecker's column of three Humvees, which is where the first fatality occurred as Dominick Pilla was killed by a single shot to the head.

The initial operation was intended to last an hour but turned into an overnight battle and rescue operation that saw 18 American soldiers killed and 73 wounded. Still to this day, the exact number of Somali casualties is unknown, but estimates range from several hundred to over a thousand with injuries to another 3,000–4,000.

The Plan

Delta operators were to assault the target building (using Little Bird helicopters) and secure the targets inside the building while four Ranger chalks (under CPT Michael D. Steele's command) were to fast-rope down from circling MH-60L Black Hawk helicopters. The Rangers were then to create a four-corner defensive perimeter around the target building, while a column of nine HMMWVs and three M939 five-ton trucks (under LTC Danny McKnight's command) would arrive at the building to take the entire assault team and their prisoners back to base. The entire operation was estimated to take no longer than 30 minutes.

However, the ground-extraction convoy was delayed and found itself under attack by Somali citizens and local militia, who also blocked its path by forming barricades in the streets with Aidid supporters using megaphones to encourage the local population to come onto the streets and defend their homes.

First Black Hawk

The first Black Hawk downed, callsign Super 61, was CW3 Cliff "Elvis" Wolcott's bird. Both he and co-pilot CW3 Donovan Briley were killed in the crash and the two crew chiefs were severely wounded, but both Delta snipers survived and began defending the site.

CW3 Karl Maier's and CW5 Keith Jones's MH-6, callsign Star 41, landed nearby. Jones left the helicopter while Maier provided cover and repeatedly refused orders to lift off while his co-pilot was not in the bird. Reportedly, Karl Maier's covering fire almost hit LT DiTomasso as he led his Ranger chalk to the crash site. Jones and Maier evacuated the Delta snipers from the crash site, but sadly one of

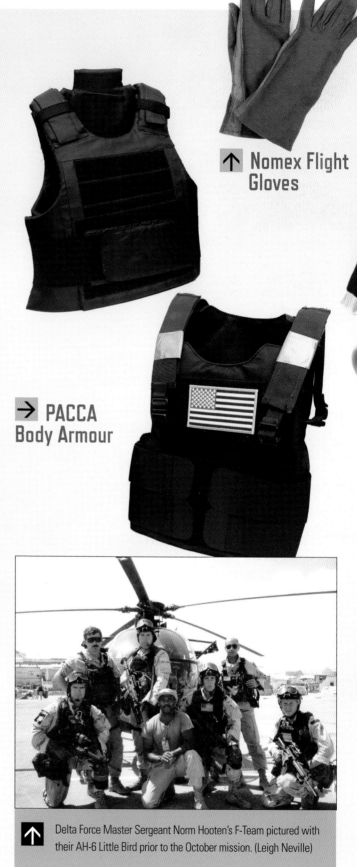

↑ **Nomex Flight Gloves**

→ **PACCA Body Armour**

↑ Delta Force Master Sergeant Norm Hooten's F-Team pictured with their AH-6 Little Bird prior to the October mission. (Leigh Neville)

them later died of his injuries as he was shot four times while trying to protect the downed helicopter and its surviving crew.

A Combat Search and Rescue (CSAR) team, led by Delta Operator CAPT Bill J. Coultrup and Air Force Pararescueman MSGT Scott C. Fales, were able to fast-rope down to Super 61's crash site despite an RPG hit that crippled their helicopter, Super 68, piloted by CW3 Dan Jollota, who managed to limp his crippled bird back to base. The CSAR team found both the pilots dead and two crew chiefs wounded inside the crashed helicopter.

Under crazy fire from all directions, the team moved the wounded to a nearby collection point, where they built a makeshift shelter using Kevlar armour plates salvaged from Super 61's wreckage.

Meanwhile the "fog of war" had descended amongst the ground convoy and the assault team, which cost them both valuable time as both waited for each element to contact each other, which was a costly mistake that isn't, by the way, covered or explained in the film. The only thing that saved the well dug in troops at crash site one from repeated Somali attacks was the strafing and rocket attacks from circling Little Birds piloted by crews from the "Night Stalkers", which at the time where the only air unit equipped and trained for night fighting.

Second Black Hawk

During the wait, a second Black Hawk helicopter, callsign Super 64 – CW3 Michael Durant's bird – was shot down by an RPG round, but because most of the ground force went to the aid of the first crashed bird Mike Durant's bird was unprotected other than by two Delta snipers, MSG Gary Gordon and SFC Randy Shughart, who dropped down from Super 64's wingman, Super 62. They inflicted heavy casualties on the approaching Somali mob with the help of air support from Super 62, who also took an RPG hit and reluctantly had to return to base.

Both Gordon and Shughart were killed, reportedly by headshots. This provoked the US Special Forces community into re-evaluating their love affair with non-ballistic helmets. With the deaths of both Delta snipers, the Somalis overran the crash site killing everyone but Durant, who was nearly beaten to death but then saved by Aidid's men who took him as their prisoner. For their actions, MSG Gordon and SFC Shughart were posthumously awarded the Medal of Honor, the first award of the medal since the Vietnam War.

→ **Lightweight Chest Rig**

↓ **US Desert Boots**

THE 1ST SPECIAL FORCES OPERATIONAL DETACHMENT – DELTA (1ST SFOD-D)

Known simply as Delta or CAG (Combat Applications Group), the unit is an elite special missions unit, which falls under the operational control of JSOC. Tasked with hostage rescue and counter-terrorism, as well as direct action and special reconnaissance against high-value targets, it is the US military's primary counter-terrorism unit.

The majority of Delta Force operators are selected from the US Army Special Operations Command's elite Special Forces Groups and the 75th Ranger Regiment. Delta Force was formed as a direct result of well-publicised terrorist incidents in the 1970s.

Delta Force's structure is thought to be based on the UK's Special Air Service and Delta is reported to have a core force of around 1,000 soldiers, with c.300 of them trained to conduct direct action and hostage rescue operations. The remaining personnel are highly specialised support personnel who are among the very best in their fields.

HOLLYWOOD VS THE REAL WORLD

One of the most recognisable and iconic loadouts to ever find its way onto the skirmish field is that of the Delta contingent of Task Force Ranger, but as with the majority of gear that finds its way onto a Hollywood film set, there are subtle differences between the real world and what appears on the "silver screen". There are often good reasons for these discrepancies, with some kit simply not being available, but in this case the commercial world took over as the tactical mega brand Blackhawk were all over the film and used their equipment where they could.

The uniform of choice at the time was the new American Desert three-colour Battle Dress Uniform (BDU) or Desert Combat Uniform (DCU). It was first seen in 1991 and was issued en masse to the US Army in 1992, just before Task Force Ranger deployed. It would be fair to say that the whole of Delta was issued and used "Tri-Color". The same can't be said for the 3rd Battalion, 75th Ranger Regiment as pictures of the time clearly show Rangers wearing a mixture of "Tri-Color" and six-colour desert camouflage "chocolate-chip camouflage" clothing. The film very cleverly depicted the changeover in camouflage, by using a combination of "Tri-Color" clothing and chocolate-chip camouflage helmet covers and boonie hats.

The US Army Special Forces' use of "bump helmets" was a controversial decision at the time. However, there was a real need for a lighter, more manoeuvrable helmet and none were available. The deaths of MSG Gordon and SFC Shughart by headshots set in motion a whole new direction in the development of SOF headgear that offered the user lightweight flexibility with a decent level of ballistic protection.

The film shows Delta wearing Pro-Tec "High Cut" Classics, but in reality both the high and full cut helmets were used. Both helmets would have been fitted with ANVIS 6 NVG mounts and battery packs and worn in conjunction with Bolle X500 goggles and a Setcom 5 headset. The only problem here is that you are not going to be able to find the majority of these items, other than perhaps the Bolle X500, and if you do they are going to cost you a small fortune. This is the probable reason the film used a number of different options instead.

The two most common sets of goggles worn were Oakley L-Frames in matte black and USGI Sand, Wind and Dust goggles; the other option we have for you is a goggle manufactured by Aim Top called SF500 Goggles. These are a pretty good take on Bolle's X500 but at half the price; however, if you want the realism of the X500, you can find a number of retailers stocking them online. The helmet itself is very difficult to find and again this is the probable reason it wasn't used in the film. A quick search online will find skate helmets in the shape you are looking for and again at a fraction of the price of the branded versions.

Delta's DCU shirts have clearly received a "raid mod" in that the pockets have been removed from the chest and reattached to the shoulders with the addition of black Velcro strips; while the majority of pocket flaps were left clear some of the Delta operators added their blood group to this area.

Despite a lot of misinformation online, raid modding is nothing new. In fact, the 101st Airborne modified their uniform shirts during World War II as did soldiers in Vietnam. This mod was simply a way of making pockets more accessible while wearing body armour, which some 73 years on from the first mods made during World War II has become a standard design on combat shirts the world over.

REALISM OVER COMMERCIALITY

I wonder how many times you have watched a war movie and spotted errors in the clothing, gear and tactics – we do it all the time. Sadly the film *Black Hawk Down* starts to fall apart with the Delta gear from this point on. We suspect the realism took a back seat to the commercial world as mega brand Blackhawk flooded the wardrobe department with as much of their gear as they could to brush aside the competitive brands that were actually used on the real operation. In the real world, Delta's preferred body armour supplier was a company called TG Faust, which sadly doesn't exist anymore, though the common assumption is that PT body armour was used. At a glance the Faust vest looks like a slimmed-down version of a set of PT armour, which was way ahead of its time in terms of functionality. However, for us a better option – and slightly closer to the Faust – would be the PACCA armour. In reality whichever plate carrier you chose you're going to have to do some work to both plate carriers as they need more Velcro coverage to bring them in line with the Faust version, plus two buckle loops situated at the front of the plate carrier to integrate an AWS Industries Strike Chest Rig, which can also be found on the replica market at great prices. However, if the film is to be believed, the on-screen characters would have been issued with PT Armour and Blackhawk chest rigs, load-bearing vest and tactical vests, and sometimes a combination of all three.

The same can be said about the belt order that was used in the film and the apparent use of ALICE gear by the Delta assault teams. Yes, they did use the odd pouch, but nowhere as much as the filmmakers will have you believe. Interestingly, members of the 75th Ranger Regiment were known to have worn a version of the Faust body armour, over which they wore full sets of ALICE gear.

The most popular holster used by Delta at the time was the Safariland 3004, which can still be purchased today from a number of US online retailers at a reasonable price, but if you don't want the added expense you can pick up a replica holster at a fraction of the cost and alter its appearance by adding a leg and belt strap or even go for the Blackhawk Omega holsters used in the film. The belt itself would have been a simple duty belt with a quick release buckle, which again is quite easy to source.

The final pieces of the puzzle are knee pads, boots and gloves, which again are entirely different to what was shown in the film, with the exception of the gloves. The exact knee pads were produced by Bike USA and as far as we know have gone out of production, but for the sake of completing this loadout, we went for a set of modern Alta pads, which again feature in the film and can easily be found with many online retailers stocking them. The boots were a simple desert boots and not the Adidas GSG9s that were featured in the film. It would be remiss of us not to mention that Delta was issued with GSG9s, but for the most part as far as we can tell desert boots were by far the most common Delta footwear used at the time.

The gloves are a simple pair of Nomex flight gloves, which are easily sourced, hard wearing and close-fitting. They will offer you minimal protection on a skirmish field from natural hazards and finish off your Delta Force loadout.

RANGERS LEAD THE WAY

The 75th Ranger Regiment is a light infantry airborne special operations force that is part of the US Army Special Operations Command. The primary mission of the regiment is to conduct direct action raids in hostile or sensitive environments worldwide. Other skill sets of the Rangers include airfield seizure, special reconnaissance, personnel recovery and recon missions. The regiment can deploy one Ranger battalion within 18 hours of being placed on alert.

Hollywood seems to have nailed the Ranger on-screen presence – there were a few discrepancies, such as the use of black Faust body armour and a larger presence of "chocolate-chip camouflage" than necessary, but this iconic loadout was pretty much there. This one is easy to reproduce on the skirmish field using real-world products and the odd cost-effective replica for hard-to-find original gear.

Helmet

Hated by the Special Forces community of the time, the Personnel Armour System for Ground Troops or PASGT Helmet was heavy and cumbersome. Designed in the mid-1970s as a replacement for the M1, prototypes of the PASGT were tested in the late 1970s before being issued in the 1980s. In the early 2000s, the PASGT was eventually replaced. Because of its wide use across the US military you can easily pick up a good condition "K-pot" from a number of online retailers across the globe; however, if you don't want the added weight of the helmet on the skirmish field, there are a number of plastic replicas, which are a fraction of the cost of a real "K-pot" and once you have a cover over the helmet there really is no way of telling the difference unless you're up close and personal.

All of the Rangers deployed on Task Force Ranger were also issued with a set of USGI Sand, Wind and Dust goggles and a chocolate-chip camouflage boonie hat, which was worn on the base and which can be seen in the film several times.

DCU

We'll forget that there was an amount of chocolate-chip camouflage still used by the Rangers at this point and concentrate on what was pretty much the newly issued three-colour DCU; however, this time it's straight out of the quartermaster's stores and not raid modified.

Interestingly, desert soil samples from the Middle East were used to create the camouflage colour palette and then tested in Saudi Arabia and Kuwait. By 1992, the first wide-scale issue of DCUs was supplied to the US Army and by the end of 1995, all three arms of the American armed forces had been issued with DCUs.

Ranger Body Armour

The RBA was a very unique piece of kit designed especially for the 75th Ranger Regiment and was issued from the 1990s through to the early 2000s.

Early versions of RBA which only had front armour first saw active service in Operation *Gothic Serpent*. This limited protection resulted in serious injury and/or death for some of the Rangers in Somalia. SGT James Joyce was killed by a single gunshot wound to his back.

At least two major variations of RBA were produced in the real world. The first variant used only a front rigid ballistic armour plate and an unmodified nylon fabric carrier. The second variant used both a front and a back ballistic armour plate, and a small storage pocket to the front ballistic plate pocket, and featured nylon equipment retention straps on each shoulder. The second version was rushed into production after the injuries and deaths in Somalia.

Replicas are easier to find than you might think and include the correct version with only a front plate pocket.

→ Para cord

← Ranger Body Armour replica

↑ DCU Teesar three-colour uniform

↓ Plastic PASGT Helmet

ALICE GEAR

The All-Purpose Lightweight Individual Carrying Equipment load-bearing system was first issued to the US Army as far back as 1973. ALICE gear was the result of the LINCLOE (Lightweight Individual Clothing and Equipment) program that came to life in 1965. The goal of the individual equipment part of the LINCLOE program was to develop a lightweight load-carrying system to lighten a combat soldier's overall load. The ALICE system fighting load comprises the following components:

- Belt, Individual Equipment, LC-1 (NSN 8465-00-001-6487)
- Carrier, Entrenching Tool, LC-1 (NSN 8465-00-001-6474)
- Case, Field First Aid Dressing, LC-1 (NSN 8465-00-935-6814)
- Case, Small Arms Ammunition, LC-1 (NSN 8465-00-001-6482)
- Cover, Water Canteen, LC-1 (NSN 8465-00-860-0256)
- Suspenders, Individual Equipment Belt, LC-1 (NSN 8465-00-001-6471)

Belt, Individual Equipment

The individual equipment belt is constructed of US Army Shade 7 olive drab nylon webbing with a black chemical finish, adjusting buckles, keepers, and a belt buckle. The medium size individual equipment belt (NSN 8465-00-001-6488) is for soldiers with waists measuring under 30 inches (76cm) and size large (NSN 8465-00-001-6487) is for those with waists measuring 30 inches (76cm) or over. The individual equipment belt is adjusted from each end using clamp-type buckles which slide on the equipment belt when open. The individual equipment items are attached by interlocking belt-strap keepers or are hooked through eyelets along the bottom of the belt. The eyelets along the top of the individual equipment belt are for connecting the individual equipment belt suspenders.

In 1981 the new Belt, Individual Equipment, LC-2 was introduced with the green plastic quick-release buckle and was assigned the National Stock Number 8465-01-120-0674 (medium) and 8465-01-120-0675 (large).

Carrier, Entrenching Tool

The entrenching tool carrier is moulded of EVA, and the top flap is secured through two metal snap fasteners. It attaches to the individual equipment belt using two belt-strap keepers with interlocking slides. The entrenching tool carrier is designed to accommodate the lightweight collapsible Entrenching Tool, Hand (NSN 5120-00-878-5932).

Case, Field First Aid Dressing

The field first aid dressing case is constructed of Army Shade 106 olive green water repellent treated 7.25 ounces (206g) nylon duck. It is 8½ inches (22cm) long with the flap open; approximately 4½ inches (11cm) wide, and forms a 4-inch (10cm) deep pocket. It has a metal snap-type fastener closure and is attached to the individual equipment belt or individual equipment belt suspenders by a belt-strap keeper with an interlocking slide. The field first aid dressing case is designed to accommodate either the Dressing, First Aid, Field (NSN 6510-00-159-4883) or the Compass, Magnetic, Unmounted (NSN 6605-00-151-5337).

Case, Small Arms Ammunition

The small arms ammunition case is designed to accommodate three 30-round Magazine, Cartridge (NSN 1005-00-921-5004) used with the Rifle, 5.56 Millimeter, M16A1. It is constructed of nylon duck and webbing with polyester sheet stiffeners in the front, rear and lid of the small arms ammunition case. Each cartridge magazine is held in place by ¾-inch (1.9cm) wide webbing spacers; these cross the top of the small arms ammunition case. The lid is closed using a plastic latch. Grenade carrying pockets are located on each side of the small arms ammunition case which is secured by means of a nylon web strap and metal snap fastener. A tab with a metal eyelet is located at the top back of the small arms ammunition case to which the individual equipment belt suspenders are attached. The small arms ammunition case is connected to the individual equipment belt by belt-strap keepers with interlocking slides.

Cover, Water Canteen

The water canteen cover is fabricated of nylon cloth and webbing and acrylic pile liner material. The two-flap closure is secured by means of metal snap fasteners. There is a small pocket on the front of the cover for carrying water purification tablets. The lid of this small pocket is secured by means of hook-and-pile fastener tape. The cover attaches to the individual equipment belt by means of two belt-strap keepers with interlocking slides. The water canteen cover is designed to accommodate the Canteen, Water (NSN 8465-00-889-3477). In 1975, the LC-1 designation for the water canteen cover was changed to LC-2 due to some minor design changes. The National Stock Number remains the same.

Suspenders, Individual Equipment Belt

The individual equipment belt suspenders are Y shaped with three adjusting straps, but four points of attachment to the unique equipment belt and small arms ammunition cases. The shoulder straps are padded with spacer cloth. Each shoulder strap has a web loop and a non-slip buckle on each of the straps in the front and one at the back through which the adjusting straps pass. There are rectangular wire loops located between the web loops and the buckles on the front of the straps. The 1-inch (2.5cm) wide adjusting straps have side-retaining snap hooks at one end. The back adjusting strap has an inverted V of which each end has a side-retaining snap hook. Each of the adjusting straps has a loop around it made of 1-inch (2.5cm) elastic material. In 1991, the individual equipment belt suspenders were re designated LC-2 with no apparent modifications.

You will require the following items:

- 1 x Suspenders
- 1 x Belt
- 2 x Ammunition pouches
- 2 x Water canteen covers
- 2 x Field dressing case
- 1 x Butt pack
- 1 x Strobe pouch

Because of its mass issue the whole system is very easily tracked down and affordable; however, you may have to shop around to find the component parts, because in our experience retailers did not stock the entire system.

The final pieces of the puzzle are the same as the Delta loadout – knee pads, boots and gloves. Unlike the Delta knee pads the Rangers were issued Alta pads. Again the boots were standard issue, while the gloves would have been Nomex flight gloves and if you want to be accurate add a pair of USGI Issue Military Rappelling Heavy Duty Work Gloves to your loadout, but be prepared to hang them from your belt as they are too thick to use as a shooter's glove.

SHOPPING LIST RANGER

Plastic PASGT Helmet
Chocolate-chip camouflage cover
USGI Sun, Wind and Wust goggles
DCU Teesar three-colour uniform
US Desert Boots
Ranger Body Armour replica
ALICE yoke
ALICE belt
ALICE magazine pouch x 2
ALICE water bottle pouch x 2
ALICE butt pack (replica)
ALICE field dressing pouch
Alta Tactical Knee Pads
Nomex Flight Gloves

ADDITIONAL ITEMS
100 MPH US Military tape
Para cord
TMC Replica Stun Grenade
KM-HEAD Cotton Sling for M16 (Olive)

AVAILABLE FROM ZERO ONE AIRSOFT, MILITARY 1ST, FIRE SUPPORT, OTHER AIRSOFT RETAILERS AND EBAY MERCHANTS.

SHOPPING LIST DELTA

Matt Black BMX Skate Helmet
Bolle X500 Goggles
Aim Top SF 500 Goggles – optional
DCU Teesar three-colour uniform
PT Body Armour
PCCA Body Armour – optional
Viper LA Mesh Vest – optional
Lightweight Chest Rig
Replica AWS Chest Rig – optional
Viper Security belt
Safariland 3004
Black Hawk Omega Holster – optional
ALICE magazine pouch
ALICE water bottle pouch
ALICE field dressing pouch
Alta Tactical Knee Pads
Nomex Flight Gloves
US Desert Boots

AVAILABLE FROM ZERO ONE
AIRSOFT, MILITARY 1ST,
TAIWAN GUN, TOY SOLDIER,
OTHER AIRSOFT RETAILERS AND
EBAY MERCHANTS.

CHAPTER FOUR

SBS AT THE BATTLE FOR QALA-I-JANGHI

The Special Boat Service (SBS) has its origins in the Special Boat Section of World War II and was re-founded under the Royal Marines in 1951 as the Special Boat Company. It was renamed the Special Boat Squadron in 1974 and the Special Boat Service in 1987. It has formed a key part of the UK's Special Forces capability ever since.

The War in Afghanistan saw the SBS's most significant deployment of the 21st century. One of the key events of the SBS's initial deployment was the Battle for Qala-i-Janghi, one of the most hard-fought actions of Operation *Enduring Freedom*. The battle has also provided the subject for some of the most popular loadouts featured in *Airsoft International* and the images that accompanied the feature have gone viral with them often being confused with genuine SBS operatives. That is in part no doubt down to their great kit selection, but also down to the amazing setting of the "Spec Ops – The Rock" site in the UK.

THE SBS IN AFGHANISTAN

With the title of the "Special Boat Service" you might expect the SBS to be more at home in and around a maritime environment, but much like the US Navy SEALs, the skills of this elite fighting force have commonly been called upon in land-locked environments. Early in the war in Afghanistan, the SBS played an instrumental part in the invasion and is credited with securing Bagram Airbase which would later become the largest US military base in Afghanistan. Beyond Bagram, the Battle for Qala-i-Janghi became the subject for a great deal of media attention as one of the longest and bloodiest individual battles of the entire campaign in Afghanistan. This attention allowed for a brief glimpse at the men that formed the SBS and has since fuelled the imaginations of many enthusiasts and re-enactors.

The Uprising

Qala-i-Janghi Fort was a prisoner of war camp in northern Afghanistan, near the city of Mazar-i-Sharif. In late 2001 the fort was populated with a large number of men who had surrendered to the Afghan Northern Alliance (ANA) during fighting in the nearby city of Kunduz. The prisoners, many of whom were non-combatants, were held for interrogation by the CIA. Between 25 November and 1 December 2001 a violent revolt broke out that led to a bloody battle within the fort and the surrounding area which would take the combined efforts of the Afghan National Army as well as US and British Special Forces and air support to bring under control. It would be remembered as one of the most violent episodes of the war.

The prison was secured by a small group of ANA and US personnel, but with an estimated 500 inmates involved in the revolt and able to break into the armoury held on site and secure stockpiled weapons such as AKs and RPGs using fearsome suicide attacks, it was not long before the prisoners were organised into an armed fighting force.

Quick Reaction Force

An eight-man SBS team was nearby and able to act as a Quick Reaction Force or QRF and responded in an attempt to assist the beleaguered prison security force. The small team arrived in two armed Land Rovers to find a battle erupting around them and came under fire as they attempted to suppress the enemy forces inside the fort.

After removing the mounted GPMGs from the Land Rovers the SBS task force was able to lay down a superior amount of firepower to beat back the enemy forces as they tried to break out of the fort and escape by force. This strategic use of firepower allowed the SBS to buy enough time for further help to arrive in the form of US Special Forces and air support.

← Two SBS operators in civilian dress (to the right) work with 5th Special Forces Group personnel during the Taliban uprising at the 'Fort of War' in Mazar-i-Sharif, Afghanistan in 2001. (Oleg Nikishin/Getty Images)

CIA Rescue

Amongst the friendly security personnel battling inside the fort were two CIA Special Activities Division (SAD) officers, Johnny "Mike" Spann and Dave "Dawson" Tyson, who had arrived only days previously in order to interrogate the prisoners.

Unfortunately, Spann was killed in the fighting, but although Tyson managed to hole up in relative safety and was even able to relay messages to the friendly forces via satellite phone from inside the fort. Spann's body was eventually recovered by American forces – he was the only westerner to die in the fighting.

Over nearly a week, mounting pressure from friendly forces and strategic air assets forced the enemy fighters into the tunnels beneath the forts. At one point a 2,000-pound JDAM went off course and unfortunately hit an ANA armoured vehicle, killing friendly troops.

Eventually an ANA commander made the decision to drive out the enemy fighters from within the tunnels of the ancient fortress by simply flooding them with water. At the conclusion of the fighting only 86 prisoners remained alive out of the estimated 500 that had been to start with.

Trojan Attack

Among the 86 prisoners recaptured after the battle was one John Walker Lindh, who infamously moved to Afghanistan from America to join the Taliban prior to 9/11. An embedded journalist recognized Lindh and he was given medical treatment by a US Special Forces medic before being sent back to America to stand trial for treason. He was found guilty in 2002 and was sentenced to 20 years without parole.

Due to the high-profile figures involved and the manner in which their number had surrendered previously, some found with concealed weapons at the time, it has been speculated that the Qala-i-Janghi attack was a predetermined "trojan horse" operation, allowing for a large number of capable and committed fighters to forcibly take over an important and strategically solid position such as the fort, and the munitions stockpile within. It is perhaps due to this speculation that the force of the SBS was used to quash the efforts of the Taliban here.

RECREATING THE KIT

Bringing the equipment of the Battle of Qala-i-Janghi to the skirmish field is simple. A lot has changed since 2001 and if you are used to Multicam everything by Crye Precision, this will be something of a departure. British-based outdoor brands like Craghoppers and Karrimor were often used by soldiers operating outside the parameters of issued kit, and for good reason – the products were highly evolved for the task.

Special Forces operators also benefited from the more casual look and less overtly military appearance afforded by off-the-shelf clothing and equipment. Here we have teamed a number of items up to form a practical, wallet-friendly and capable loadout.

The trousers used are Craghoppers Kiwi walking trousers. It's been speculated that these were the actual trousers used by UK Special Forces at the time and this is certainly credible since they are a trusted favourite within outdoorsy circles. The versions we have used are perhaps slightly anachronistic since they are from 2013 but the design has changed only slightly over the years.

Craghoppers Kiwi Classic trousers features:

- Nine pockets including OS map-sized cargo pocket and five zipped security pockets
- Reinforced knee and seat
- Part-elasticated waist for comfort and fit
- Mobile phone holder
- SmartDry Nano water-repellent finish
- Belt included
- Heel tape
- SolarDry UPF40+ fabric
- Lifetime guarantee

A simple cotton long-sleeved top has been used as a base layer and depending on the climate you are playing in, this could be swapped out for something with more insulation or even just a simple T-shirt without compromising the authenticity of the look. If you are really determined to pull this loadout together whatever the weather, DPM smocks of various designs were popularly used during the early 2000s so you can adapt for all seasons.

LOAD CARRYING

If you are used to getting strapped up with a plate carrier and going the whole nine yards when it comes to load carrying, this loadout will either make for a refreshing change or you'll feel totally under-dressed! This set-up is rapidly becoming a favourite when it comes to actually playing as it's just so much less restrictive and stifling compared to most kit.

The load-carrying capacity is primarily provided by means of a tactical vest. The actual vests used by the operatives at Qala-i-Janghi were manufactured by SigPro but as time has worn on these have gradually become less and less findable. They are probably sitting hidden away at the back of a few UK gear collectors' kit cupboards! The good news is that 5.11 have had an almost identical vest in their range for some time and to all intents and purposes it's indistinguishable.

The capacity is vast with numerous large pockets capable of accepting primary and secondary weapon magazines along with extras like radios and tools in zippered and Velcro-flapped pockets. If you want MOLLE or armour carrying you've come to the wrong place here but the 5.11 tactical vest offers heaps of concealment and practical applications that actually come in devilishly handy on the field, all in a comfortable and easy-to-wear package that you can keep and wear down the shops when you are a pensioner!

5.11 Tactical Range Vest features:

- Versatile and durable
- Designed for concealed carry
- Back-up Belt System
- Reinforced half-collar
- Hidden BBS (Back-up Belt System) pockets on each side of vest
- 18 pockets
- Two pockets sized for AR Magazines
- Rear water bottle pockets
- 360-degree pocket that wraps completely around the vest
- Key hook for safe access to keys

- iPAD (Velcro Attachment Pad System) compatible
- Quad-stitched and bartacked at all stress points
- Material: two layers of 8.5oz., 100 per cent cotton canvas

If more capacity is required, which is frequently the case, you can do as we have done and add a simple canvas claymore bag – we've used a Vietnam-era one here. Another useful option is the addition of a cloth bandolier, also something of a relic in this day and age.

Extras

We've thrown in a PRC-148 radio set from Toy Soldier into the vest and used the included PTT to wire it in to a basic security earpiece. The PTT and earpiece might not be the most accurate representation of the equipment that was used at the time but thanks to the way the vest works, you can quite easily hide these items away in pouches without spoiling the look of the loadout.

The obligatory shemagh is used as face and neck coverage and if you wanted to, you could add some gloves if you require a little more protection from the elements. As far as eye protection is concerned we've used ballistic shades but this is something you should never compromise on on the skirmish field, as we know you are undoubtedly aware.

Footwear is another aspect of personal protective gear you should never skimp on but the great news is that many personnel in the early 2000s used simple civilian hiking or trekking boots and reference images even show simple rough-out issued desert boots, which are a cheap and cheerful choice.

FIREPOWER – L119

The primary armament of the UK Special Forces is the L119A1 rifle, which, despite its looks is NOT just an M4. There are subtle but important differences between the two. The replica shown here is based around a Tokyo Marui Recoil gun, which you can read about in detail on page 45 of *Airsoft Illustrated* Volume 10 Issue 5.

Strangely, the process of building an L119 from a regular AEG basis has not changed much in the six years since we've been looking at this subject. There's STILL nothing widely available out of the box! (Let's not even consider G&P's frankly laughable effort.)

In the past we have advised the following, which remains as true as ever: "To start with you'll need an AEG as a platform, for this an M4 RIS is ideal as it comes with a sliding stock and RIS unit, which will save buying them. However you need to make sure that it is a variant with the old-style CAR-15 sliding stock, otherwise you'll end up having to buy another." The parts you'll need to get the L119A1 looking just right are:

FIREPOWER – GPMG

British forces, amongst others, commonly use the GPMG or General Purpose Machine Gun. Visually very similar to the M240 used by American forces, the GPMG, designated the L7, does still have distinct and particular differences. Likely the centrepiece of any UK Special Forces enthusiast's collection, an accurate L7 replica is very, very difficult to get hold of in a complete state and even the correct parts can be very hard to obtain. If you are interested in owning one, we'd advise you get in touch with Fire Support, www.fire-support.co.uk.

1: L119A1 SFW Barrel Assembly

DyTac, ArmyCode and Warlord Tactical are a few manufacturers you can look to for this. The longer, 16-inch barrel is the one we have used here.

2: Storm/Stowaway Grip

The bulkier grip is characteristic of the L119A1, G&P and Guarder replicas that are just right, the G&P perhaps slightly pipping the Guarder model to the post.

3: Rubber Stock Pad

Guarder, G&P and Warlord Tactical all make serviceable replica parts to fulfil this role. If you are willing to put the time in looking for it, the genuine Diemaco one is out there, but it's very hard to get.

4: Sling Loop

Warlord Tactical again are a great place to look for the correct pattern of sling loop, although G&P and King Arms make very good versions, which are listed as either a Type 2 or Type B.

5: An L119A1-traded Receiver

With the growing popularity of UK Special Forces loadouts, the L119 receiver set is becoming easier to find, whether factory made or custom engraved. Make sure you pick up the correct Diemaco "D" marked version and not the Canadian Forces one though.

6: Front Sight

Always a cause for contention is the reinforced front sight. On the 16-inch barrel L119, the sight post is most commonly built up and the easiest place to track down one of these parts is currently Warlord Tactical. On the shorter 10-inch variant, a simple M4 sight with the bayonet lug removed will generally suffice.

CHAPTER FIVE

OLD-SCHOOL FORCE RECON

Swift, Silent, Deadly

Featuring Dave Porter

US Marine Corps Force Recon detachments perform both deep reconnaissance and direct action (DA) operations. Some missions are now shared by MARSOC, whose members were recruited from Force Recon platoons following MARSOC's establishment in 2006. As their roles have been split Force Recon can now focus on what they do best – intelligence gathering as well as Visit, Board, Search and Seizure oprerations at sea. Operating independently behind enemy lines, Force Recon Marines perform unconventional special operations in support of conventional warfare.

Their methods of deployment are not that dissimilar to the Navy SEALs, Army Special Forces and Air Force Combat Controllers; however, Force Recon's missions and tasks do differ slightly as they are there to support Marine expeditionary and amphibious operations.

WAY BACK WHEN

Force Recon can trace its history back to World War II when Amphibious Reconnaissance Battalions performed many missions supporting the landings thorughout the Pacific Theatre.

However, today's Force Recon owes a lot to its participation in the Vietnam War, where two very different mission types emerged and are still very much in use today. Keyhole "deep reconnaissance", or green operations and Stingray "direct action" patrols, which are also known as black missions.

Keyhole patrols were designed purely around reconnaissance and surveillance, usually lightly equipped and armed with defensive weapons, whereas Stingray operations were the exact opposite with the emphasis placed on aggression, with heavily armed personnel and the ability to call in air strikes, just like your average skirmish.

The CIA's highly secretive Special Activities Division (SAD), and more specifically its elite Special Operations Group (SOG) recruited directly from Marine Force Recon. Their history goes right back to the Vietnam War where Force Recon and CIA operations were part of the same umbrella MACV-SOG organization.

Green Operations

The principal mission of Force Recon is reconnaissance, so you'll be collecting intelligence on the skirmish field and pushing deep behind the opposing team's line.

Black Operations

These operations require direct action (DA) – basically "looking for trouble". Force Recon operators usually have artillery and naval gun support, which can easily be simulated on any skirmish field. Real world examples also include the seizures and occupation of gas/oil platforms (GOPLAT) and the Visit, Board, Search, and Seizure (VBSS) of ships during Maritime Interdiction Operations (MIO), as well as calling in close air support, a vital skill exercised in DA missions learned from the Vietnam War.

After the creation of Marine Special Operations Command (MARSOC) in 2006, you would think that this would have been the beginning of the end of Marine Force Recon. The creation of this new element of the US Marines certainly did take its toll on the rank and file of Force Recon because at the same time of MARSOC's creation the 2nd Force Recon Company deactivated, with many of the most experienced men folded into the newly established Marine Special Operations Battalions. The 1st Force Recon Company also shut down the same year. The remaining Marines in both Force Recon companies folded into new "D" companies within the Division Recon Battalions, forming the Deep Reconnaissance Platoons. In total, three Force Recon companies were deactivated. However, five Recon Battalions remain very active and are now part of five Marine Divisions.

This loadout is set in 2001 where M81 woodland ruled the roost and Nomex flight suits were the only fire retardant clothing in operation.

↓ ESS Tactical Goggles

↑ Admin pouch

→ Replica flight suit

→ HEAD GEAR

There's no getting away from the distinctive outline of a MIC helmet – you can spot one at a thousand yards. As we have pinpointed the date of this project, you only really have one choice of MICH at your disposal, and that, of course, is the MICH TC-2000, which is the baseline version. There was a later 2001 version, but the "high cut" version is not the right choice for this project. If you want to go super authentic, you'll want to add either a PSV-14 NVG mount, and a pair of ESS tactical goggles. Sadly there is no getting away from the cost of these additions – at over £60.00 for the goggles alone they are not cheap. However, one way to justify the price is to adopt them as your primary eye protection. They certainly have the correct ballistic rating (STANAG 2920).

ON THE READY LINE!

The current flight suit that is used by most air forces and navies is made of Nomex, a fabric made from spun aramid that is lightweight and fire-resistant. But colour, style, and cut vary from country to country. The current model flight suit for the US military is the CWU 27/P, which is virtually identical to the flight suits used by Force Recon back in 2001.

Belt order wise we are throwing on a rigger's belt – green, black or tan, it's your choice. The go-to-belt back then would have been produced by Eagle Industries and was known as a "Mission or Operator's Gun Belt"; however, today there are a whole heap of different choices available at various price points, which is great, especially if you're on a budget. One of the problems with a rigger's belt is its inability to carry loads and you will require the help of a set of tactical suspenders, which will take all of the weight off your hips and make what is essentially your "tool belt" more comfortable.

The kit you should think about adding is a holster and a dump pouch at the very least. A drop leg panel comes in very handy to add IFARK and/or ammo pouches. Again, the drop leg panel provider would have been Eagle Industries back in the day and to be super accurate there is only one choice, but that's entirely up to you.

Pouch wise, the choice for belt order, drop leg and MBAV is Eagle all the way. The range is pretty extensive and is easily purchased from many eBay stores.

If you're following our lead, we bought six M4 pouches, a selection of utility pouches, an admin pouch and a hydration pouch. If you shop wisely, you will be surprised at how cheaply you can pick these up. Although these examples were brand new, a good quality second-hand example starts from as little as £9.00 a pouch.

This plate carrier has featured in *Airsoft International* before and the platform is essentially an Eagle Industries

↖ Nomex Gloves

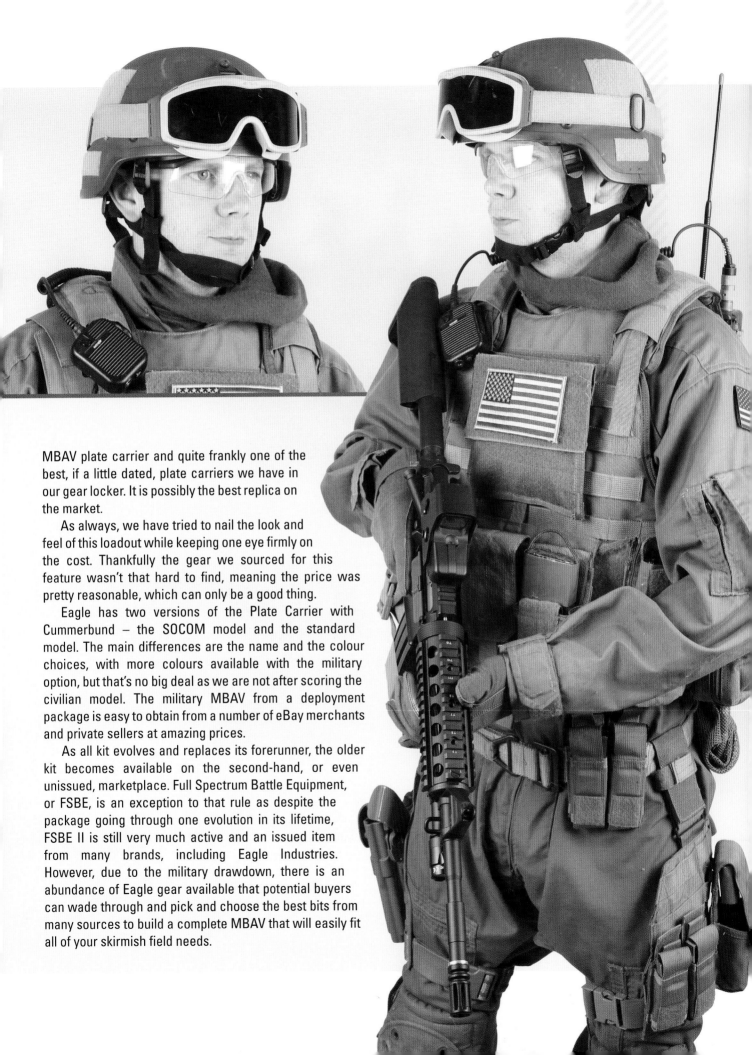

MBAV plate carrier and quite frankly one of the best, if a little dated, plate carriers we have in our gear locker. It is possibly the best replica on the market.

As always, we have tried to nail the look and feel of this loadout while keeping one eye firmly on the cost. Thankfully the gear we sourced for this feature wasn't that hard to find, meaning the price was pretty reasonable, which can only be a good thing.

Eagle has two versions of the Plate Carrier with Cummerbund – the SOCOM model and the standard model. The main differences are the name and the colour choices, with more colours available with the military option, but that's no big deal as we are not after scoring the civilian model. The military MBAV from a deployment package is easy to obtain from a number of eBay merchants and private sellers at amazing prices.

As all kit evolves and replaces its forerunner, the older kit becomes available on the second-hand, or even unissued, marketplace. Full Spectrum Battle Equipment, or FSBE, is an exception to that rule as despite the package going through one evolution in its lifetime, FSBE II is still very much active and an issued item from many brands, including Eagle Industries. However, due to the military drawdown, there is an abundance of Eagle gear available that potential buyers can wade through and pick and choose the best bits from many sources to build a complete MBAV that will easily fit all of your skirmish field needs.

POUCHES MAKE A VEST!

FSBE II has a massive assortment of pouches neatly packaged up in a deployment package – everything an operator will need and then some. This may be more than you will ever need on a skirmish field, but it's good to have options, which you can tailor to your specific needs and budget.

The most popular and least expensive are:

- M4 magazine pouches
- Pistol magazine pouches
- Respirator pouch
- Admin pouch
- Drop leg platforms
- Hydration/breaching tool pouches
- Utility pouches

However, some items enter the crazy world of the so-called "collectors' market", which artificially pushes the prices up, making them out of reach for most Airsofters.

All of the MOLLE is double stitched to handle the weight of real-world pouch attachments and their contents. The shoulder straps are box stitched for security. The MBAV is adjustable at both the shoulders and waist via the cummerbund, which can be removed entirely to streamline the carrier, but leaves you with a minimal platform and limited pouch hanging space.

The cummerbund uses a lace retention system, which gives you ample girth adjustment to a certain point, though the vest is not suitable for XXXL-sized players.

A "kangaroo pouch" sits behind the security flap, which secures the cummerbund at the front of the vest. Intended initially to holster a pistol, which can be achieved by adding a holster insert, and which was an operational requirement for vehicle-mounted members of the US Marine Corps, if you don't fancy housing your pistol there this pouch works well as a very secure utility pouch.

The back platform is big enough to secure a hydration pouch and to be honest unless you're part of a well-oiled team you won't want much else on your back.

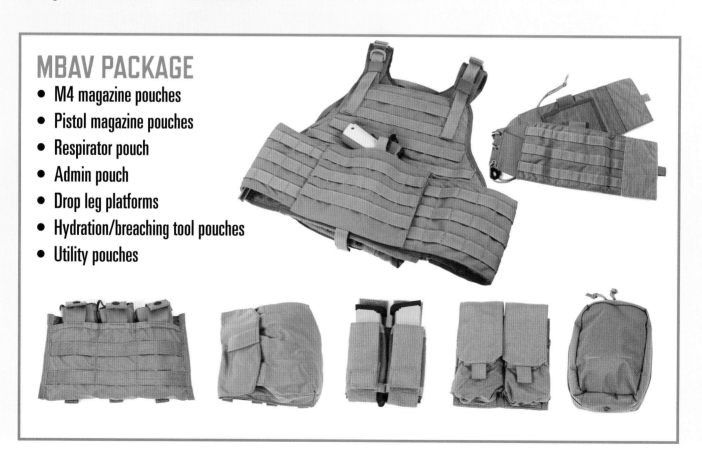

MBAV PACKAGE
- M4 magazine pouches
- Pistol magazine pouches
- Respirator pouch
- Admin pouch
- Drop leg platforms
- Hydration/breaching tool pouches
- Utility pouches

SHOPPING LIST

- Authentic MICH cover (optional)
- Replica MICH cover (optional)
- Replica helmet night vision mount
- ESS Tactical Goggles
- Replica MICH TC-2000
- Flight suit
- Bijan Woodland Knee Pads
- Rigger's belt
- Nomex gloves
- Eagle Drop Leg panel
- Tactical Thigh Holster (optional)

CHAPTER SIX

SPECIAL AIR SERVICE REGIMENT

Featuring Dave Porter

Founded in 1957 with close ties to the British SAS, this elite Australian Special Forces group has seen action in Borneo, Vietnam, Somalia, East Timor, Iraq and Afghanistan. Supporting the Australian Defence Force, the SASR also provides a native counter-terrorist capability and has sadly been called into action far too many times in Australia. Their unique capabilities also include special recovery operations, advisory and training assistance, special reconnaissance, precision strikes and direct action, but the SASR really come into their own as a covert long-range reconnaissance and surveillance force.

IN THE BEGINNING

Drawing on experiences learnt during World War II, the SASR owe a lot to Z and M Special Units, the Independent Companies and the Coastwatchers who operated in the South-west Pacific taking on the might of the Imperial Japanese Army. These units were soon disbanded after the end of World War II as part of the demobilization of the Australian military; however, after the British SAS was re-formed during the Malayan Emergency in the 1950s the Australian Army rethought its (some would say) short-sighted demobilization policy and activated its own SAS.

The 1st Special Air Service Company was established on 25 July 1957 with a total of 16 officers and 144 other ranks. In 1960, the company became part of the Royal Australian Regiment (RAR) and was given the responsibility for commando and special forces operations. As part of the organisation adopted by the Australian Army, the regiment's primary wartime role was reconnaissance. On 20 August 1964, the SAS gained regimental status and was expanded to two sabre squadrons and a headquarters, severing the link with the RAR. The third squadron was approved on 30 April 1965 as part of an overall expansion of the Australian Army.

Baptism

A whole five years had passed since the early stages of the creation of the SASR when it was called into action as part of the British Commonwealth forces stationed in North Borneo during the Indonesian Confrontation. The SASR would operate alongside its British and New Zealand counterparts in Operation *Claret*, stopping Indonesian infiltration into Malaysia. One squadron conducted reconnaissance patrols and cross-border operations in Sarawak from February to July 1965. This is where the unit had its first fatality, but no one would have suspected this as the trooper was killed by an elephant. The unit saw its second and third fatalities, but again not from any direct action – but in this case, two troopers drowned during a river crossing.

Despite often being deployed in the reconnaissance role, the SASR reportedly killed at least 20 Indonesian soldiers in a series of ambushes and contacts.

Vietnam

Fast-forward one year the SASR was deployed to the Ba Ria–Vung Tau Province of Vietnam, where it was tasked with providing intelligence to both the 1st Australian Task Force (1 ATF) and US forces, operating throughout Phuoc Tuy as well as Bien Hoa, Long Khanh and Binh Tuy provinces. The SASR squadrons rotated through Vietnam on year-long deployments, with each of the three sabre squadrons completing two tours before the last squadron was withdrawn in 1971.

While in the country the SASR performed medium-range reconnaissance patrols, observation and long-range offensive operations and ambushes.

Operating in small groups of four to six men, they moved more slowly through the bush than conventional infantry as they were heavily armed. This gave them the appearance of being a much bigger force when they were in contact.

The SASR worked closely with the New Zealand SAS, with a troop being attached to each Australian squadron from late 1968. Completing its final tour in October 1971, 2 Squadron was disbanded on return to Australia, with training squadrons being formed in its place. During its time in Vietnam, the SASR proved themselves in more ways than one and became known as the "phantoms of the jungle" due to their stealth. In a six-year period the Australian and New Zealand SAS in Vietnam conducted nearly 1,200 patrols and inflicted heavy casualties on the Viet Cong, including 492 killed, 106 possibly killed, 47 wounded, ten possibly wounded and 11 prisoners captured. Their own losses totalled one killed in action, one died of wounds, three accidentally killed, one missing and one death from illness. Twenty-eight men were wounded. During the period of its deployment, 580 men served in the SASR in Vietnam. Some members of the regiment also served with MACV-SOG units, with soldiers often serving on exchange with American Special Forces.

→ (SAAV) South African Assault Vest

Kuwait

Jumping forward some 33 years Operation *Desert Thunder* saw the SASR deploy its first squadron-strength force since Vietnam. The force was known as Anzac Special Operations Force (ANZAC SOF). The SASR was fully integrated with the New Zealand SAS and the force's role was one of Combat Search and Rescue (CSAR) of aircrew and pilots, but thankfully its services were never called upon.

They operate in small patrols of between five and six operators and are tasked with infiltrating enemy-held territory, where they provide vital on the ground reconnaissance and fire support, calling in air strikes on enemy targets. SASR patrols may also conduct sabotage and short-duration raids on high-value targets, including headquarters and airfields. All these activities can, within reason, be simulated on any skirmish field anywhere in the world.

Afghanistan

In October 2001, the Australian government announced that it was sending a Special Forces task group built around an SASR squadron to participate in the campaign against al-Qaeda and the Taliban in Afghanistan designated Operation *Slipper*. The SASR's main role in Afghanistan was to conduct reconnaissance and surveillance of al-Qaeda and Taliban positions, activities and capabilities. SASR force elements also conducted some offensive operations. After arriving at FOB Rhino, the SASR initially operated in southern Afghanistan with US Marines from Task Force 58, conducting long-range vehicle-mounted patrols over several hundred kilometres around Kandahar and into the Helmand Valley near the Iranian border.

The SASR then moved to eastern Afghanistan where it played a key role in Operation *Anaconda* in March 2002. During the operation, SASR teams were to provide in-depth operational intelligence and reconnaissance after they infiltrated the Shahi-Kot Valley ten days before the operation. They also saved the lives of 24 soldiers of the US 75th Ranger Regiment after their helicopter was shot down, by providing sniper overwatch and guiding in precise air strikes to end the enemy advance as they attempted to overrun the isolated Americans. Up to 300 al-Qaeda fighters were later estimated to have been killed as a result of the airstrikes. Two SASR advisory and liaison officers were attached to the US 10th Mountain Division to help plan the division's air assault operations and were subsequently involved in heavy fighting after the unit they were with became pinned down and took many casualties. Supported by heavy close air support they were evacuated by a helicopter that evening.

→ DISRUPTIVE PATTERN CAMOUFLAGE UNIFORM

Known as Auscam or jellybean camo, this was the original five-colour pattern used by the Australian Defence Force from the late 1970s and early 1980s. Sadly, DPCU was eventually replaced by the Australian Multicam Camouflage Uniform (AMCU), which uses an Australian-designed multi-camouflage pattern based on the US Multicam.

The first uniforms went on test in 1983 and issued in 1986. DPCU was developed following aerial photographs of the Australian terrain, which ultimately determined the colour plait for what is essentially a five-colour pattern. The final five-colour pattern consists of a greenish sand coloured background with randomly arranged spots of orange-brown, mid-brown, leaf-green and very dark green

→ DISRUPTIVE PATTERN DESERT UNIFORM

First seeing the light of day in 1998, DPDU was rushed into production in 2001 for the SASR's first deployment Afghanistan.

A second version from a year later used five colours: brown, lime green, grey, and a very light blue on a tan background. This was again issued to the SASR in Afghanistan after the first version was found to be too light in colour for the terrain. This was followed by a third issue in brown, grey, very light blue and purple on a yellow background. The cut was changed in the shirt with the bottom pockets being removed and placed on the sleeves in the "raid" style of US BDUs. A fourth version went into production in 2006 and was the last time that this unique and distinctive pattern was used.

The one thing you have to be careful about with this particular loadout is the timeline as the version of DPDU you choose will really define what gear to wear. Early deployments to Afghanistan saw the SASR wearing

primitive gear in comparison to today's standards, which bizarrely for us is a good thing and much easier and therefore cheaper to source. Later deployments saw the SASR get into the tactical gear "groove" with very specific gear being issued from the likes of Platatac and SORD, which will command a hefty price on the second-hand market.

→ GETTING INTO THE GROOVE

The more you research the SASR's deployments to Afghanistan the more you'll find yourself straying off the tactical gear beaten track, with brands such as Hellweg and designations such as ISAPO throwing curve balls at you, but thankfully the timeline of some of this kit is way past where we want to be with the loadout. It was a simple time, when names like Eagle and LBT appeared along with SAAVs and Patrol Vests, and, if you dig deep enough, US ALICE and DCU will make the odd appearance. Of course, we have done this for a reason: affordability is, without doubt, the main draw to any loadout we undertake. If you will, it's an introduction to a specific theme – we'll point you in a rough direction, but what you decide to do from that point is up to you.

DPDU isn't that difficult to find at the right price and with a little bit of imagination you'll soon be in the SASR groove and wearing something that's pretty unique on the skirmish field. It was commonplace for the SASR to mix and match their clothing. It was quite simply what was available and what they could find in other nations' stores, especially when it came to Extended Cold Weather Clothing – there are enough pictures online to confirm this, with US DCU parkas being amongst the most used piece of "borrowed kit".

US Army Tri-Color DCU Goretex ECWCS Parka

KEEPING IT REALLY SIMPLE

Using the base and entry point of a set of used DPDU is the easy bit. For this loadout we have jumped in our battlefield time machine and enlisted the help of possibly the best known of all patrol vests, the SAAV (South African Assault Vest), which is still going strong today, some 30 years after its deployment with the then South African Defence Force.

The P83 Vest was used in 1983 to replace the then outdated Pattern 70 webbing used by the SADF and is still used today by the South African National Defence Force. Over the years there have been many changes made to the vest both on the commercial and custom front, but the original design has stayed pretty much the same. At the time of its launch, the vest was seen as being way ahead of its time and was adopted by many nations' Special Forces. The SASR was reportedly particularly fond of the vest, which resulted in many sabre squadrons wearing the vest in Afghanistan. It's plain to see why the vest was so popular. Its pre-placed pouches were in the perfect configuration for access, while their number gave the user enough storage for battlefield essentials. You only have to take a look online to see how many different manufacturers produce a version. In its own right, the vest is a pretty popular entry-level vest on the skirmish field that's certainly here to stay in whatever configuration you use it.

The SAAV was also very similar in design to a chest rig that was issued to the Australian Army in the 90s under the Land 125 system, which was and still is their primary load-bearing system, which is currently in its fourth phase of design and issue.

If the SAAV isn't your thing then there are a few other options you can add to the pile. The first is a common or garden plate carrier from the LBT stable. The LBT-0290D is an enhanced M4 Chest Harness, which was a very popular rig used by the US Special Forces. Again, it's a very simple rig that is similar in construction to a whole heap of chest rigs from that era. There are four individual pouches, and each one features Velcro closures and will hold three M-16, three AK-17 or two M-14 mags. There is a small amount of webbing at both sides where users can add additional ALICE pouches.

There are/were two forms of plate carriers that were used on the SASR's first deployment to Afghanistan. The first was the Interim Small Arms Protective Overvest, which was first seen in 1999, but you're not going to be able to find one of these ultra-rare pieces of kit. The second is a very sought-after collector's item and is the Platypus DPCU Special Forces body armour. The reason we mention it is because it's almost identical to the TG Faust body armour worn by Delta in the Battle of Mogadishu.

TOP COVER

Knowing that the timeline for this loadout is around 2001, there are a number of helmet options that would fit and were certainly used in theatre.

The MICH TC-2000/1 is one helmet that springs to mind. In both low and high cuts, both helmets would have been raw (without covers) and more often than not sprayed with desert-coloured paint. Another option if helmets are your thing is a Protec Helmet, again sprayed to a desert colour to suit your own taste, and very popular with the SASR for vehicle-mounted operations.

- **Disruptive Pattern Desert Uniform**
- **LBT-0290D Chest Rig**
- **PT armour**
- **Replica MICH**
- **Protec Helmet**
- **SAAV**

Available from Military 1st and a number of eBay merchants.

CHAPTER SEVEN

KOMMANDO SPEZIALKRÄFTE

Featuring **Dave Porter**

The Kommando Spezialkräfte (KSK) is a German Special Forces unit selected from the ranks of the German armed forces, or Bundeswehr, and tasked and deployed under Germany's Division Schnelle Kräfte (Rapid Forces Division). The KSK is highly decorated and its operators are frequently requested for joint anti-terror operations across the globe, with the majority of their work being in the Balkans and the Middle East.

Today's KSK operators fall into that all too familiar "Multicam" pile that so many countries' Special Forces groups and armies have adopted. But let's jump back in time to when KSK operators were recognised for the Flecktarn they wore, which wasn't exclusive to the German armed forces and was the launch pad for many different camouflage patterns.

KOMMANDO SPEZIALKRÄFTE

Until the creation of the KSK the German government assigned all counter-terrorist and special operations activities to the GSG 9, a highly trained police force. The German armed forces did have some units that were classed as Special Forces groups, such as the army's *Fernspäher* (Long-Distance Reconnaissance), the navy's *Kampfschwimmer* (Combat Swimmers/"Frogmen"), and (until 1989) the *Sonderwaffenbegleitkompanien* (Special Weapons Escort Companies). The creation of the KSK in 1997, saw all but one *Fernspähkompanie* fold into the ranks of the KSK.

The KSK has deployed and engaged in numerous anti-terror campaigns across the globe, including in Kosovo, Bosnia and Herzegovina and, most recently, Afghanistan.

During the War in Afghanistan, the KSK fell under the command of the International Security Assistance Force and carried out numerous operations in Kabul. It was particularly active in the American-led Task Force K-Bar.

As with all Special Forces activities, the vast majority of information about the KSK is highly classified and some is even hidden from the German Military Command. What we do know is that the KSK is a Regular Army unit at brigade level at least and divided into two battalion-sized groups: the Operational

Forces and Support Forces. The Operational Forces are divided into four commando companies, with around 100 operators.

Each of the four commando companies has five specialized platoons, each with a unique speciality and ability that can be deployed dependent upon the mission parameters:

1st Platoon: vehicle insertion
2nd Platoon: airborne insertion
3rd Platoon: amphibious operations
4th Platoon: operations in special geographic or meteorological surroundings (desert, jungle, mountain or arctic regions)
5th Platoon: reconnaissance, intelligence operations and sniper/counter-sniper operations

The elite nature of the KSK initially only allowed for German Army officers and NCOs to apply for selection. However, that criteria has now been relaxed, allowing enlisted personnel and also civilians the opportunity to apply for selection. All candidates must complete an 18-month long-range surveillance training course before the KSK considers an individual for selection.

← A German KSK operator with 5.56x45mm Heckler & Koch G36K equipped with EOTech optic. (Thomas Trutschel/Photothek via Getty Images)

FLECKTARN

Originally designed for European battlefields, Flecktarn can feature as few as three colours or as many as six. However, the most popular is a five-colour variant consisting of dark green, light green, black, red-brown and green-brown or tan depending on the supplier. The three-colour version was designed for desert conditions.

The German Army started playing around with camouflage patterns well before World War II, in fact as early as the late 1920s. However, it wasn't issued in any significant numbers until 1931. Fast-forward to 1975 and Germany developed a number of prototype camouflage patterns to replace their solid grey uniforms. "Dots" or "points", "ragged leaf" and "saw tooth edge", along with a winter variant based on pine needles, were all put into the mix. Designed by Marquardt & Schulz, several patterns were developed and tested. Eventually, a pattern named "Flecktarn B" was chosen and approved for use.

The word Flecktarn is formed from the German words Fleck (spot, blot, patch or pattern) and Tarnung (camouflage). Surprisingly some 15 years passed before the German military deployed its new camouflage pattern to its troops.

Today Flecktarn is worn by the Heer (Army), the Luftwaffe (Air Force) and some Marine (Navy) units as well as the Sanitätsdienst (Medical Service). Its official name is 5 Farben-Tarndruck der Bundeswehr.

TROPENTARN

1993 saw the German military first trial desert camouflage, the officially named 3 Farben-Tarndruck der Bundeswehr (three-colour camouflage print of the Bundeswehr). Tropentarn remained on trial right up until 1999. In 2004 another version of Tropentarn was issued to German Special Forces, and this is the one which would have been used in Afghanistan. A commercial version was also available, which meant that this new Special Forces exclusive camouflage could be purchased by members of the Regular Army and worn on deployment. Consisting of clusters of pinkish-grey and brown spots on a light tan background, this new design was intended to perform in arid regions with virtually no vegetation or plant coverage.

CLAWGEAR AVICEDA FLEECE HOODY

Clawgear, produced by NWM Technologies, is based in Hamburg, Germany and burst onto the tactical gear scene back in 2009. NWM Technologies describe themselves as offering the highest quality products at economical prices, which has been very much standard right across their range.

One of the things that set NWM Technologies/Clawgear apart from some other companies is their pricing and the ability to be ultracompetitive but still have their clothing and equipment produced in Germany. Clawgear's plan with the Aviceda Fleece was to develop a mid layer which was light and versatile, and which could be easily stowed. The Aviceda meets all these requirements perfectly. The fleece is very comfortable to wear, breathes well and is damp resistant and surprisingly lightweight, which makes it an ideal mid layer or a top jacket on warmer days. We have used this jacket in the field as well as the studio and it's the perfect mid layer to have in your gear locker. The thinness of the garment means it can be worn over the majority of base layers or combat shirts without loosening any mobility or restriction. At around £70 it's not a cheap purchase, but it works well and believe it or not is a lot less expensive than real-world brands that KSK have been known to use.

Features:

- Torso: 80 per cent cotton / 20 per cent polyester
- Sleeves, collar and shoulder area: 65 per cent cotton / 35 per cent polyester
- YKK zip
- Sizes small through to XXL

INVADER GEAR COMBAT SHIRT

This German tactical gear manufacturer was founded in 2004 with the guiding principle of producing high quality at affordable prices. Invader Gear became an instant hit with our Airsoft brothers in Europe and has started to pop up on the radar of British players over recent months, mainly offering a large selection of tactical clothing in a wide range of different colours and camouflage patterns, plus nylon gear including pouches, backpacks, protective pads, slings and much more. This brand has rapidly become a one-stop shop and was the right choice for us to compile our interpretation of KSK for this feature.

The Invader Gear Combat Shirt is an excellent example of modern kit not having to cost a fortune, with a generous range of sizes and high production values that it would seem only a German company could deliver. Designed to be worn under plate carriers or body armour, it has good moisture wicking properties. The collar features a good-quality YKK zip and can be worn open or closed. Large shoulder pockets provide quick and convenient storage and the ability to add those all-important patches. The elbows are reinforced with an additional layer of fabric, which can also take elbow pads if desired. The sleeves match the garment sizes, although the XL we had was slightly too long, easily fixed by rolling the cuffs back.

PREDATOR COMBAT TROUSERS

Predator Combat Trousers are made from a sturdy cotton polyester combination and have been produced in a ripstop material. They are also reinforced with double stitching in several high-wear, high-stress locations, which is excellent for the skirmish field.

The waistband offers a good level of comfort and is padded and slightly raised at the back to provide a snug, but flexible fit and features a band of elastic, breathable fabric, which wicks moisture and heat from your body, while adding even more flexibility when bending. The same stretchy fabric is found surrounding the knees, providing ventilation, flexibility and wicking. Both the back of the knees and ankles can be adjusted for extra comfort, giving you more or less movement in the trousers. A total of ten pockets provides more than ample storage solutions – two deep hip pockets, two small mid-thigh pockets, two large mid-thigh cargo size pockets plus an additional two small side pockets just above the ankles.

Features:

- Cotton polyester combination
- Ripstop material
- Double stitching in several high-wear, high-stress locations
- Ample pockets
- Sizes small through to XXL

REAPER PLATE CARRIER

This plate carrier is a lightweight, multifunctional low-profile carrier with extremely high production values, but a very affordable price point. Available in a number of different camo patterns, it's not typically worn by KSK as it is a specific Airsoft brand, but it is a perfect likeness to the favoured Lindnerhof-Taktik carrier that's almost four times more expensive. As with the real-world Lindnerhof carrier, the Reaper has an internal tri-mag pouch and is covered in laser-cut MOLLE, giving you more than enough real estate to position those mission-critical pouches. The top three rows are separated with lines of hook-and-loop, allowing you to attach all manner of patches, while the cummerbund is adjustable and also covered with laser-cut MOLLE holes. The shoulder straps are padded to an extent, but non-adjustable. This plate carrier is also issued with fake foam plates, which helps with its shape but can become uncomfortable very quickly.

Features:

- Ample laser-cut MOLLE
- Internal tri-mag pouch
- Adjustable cummernund
- Hook-and-loop ID panels

Available from Airsoft Zone
www.Airsoftzone.com

GETTING IT RIGHT?

This is a loaded question. There are certain absolutes in life. There is a right way to get an A in your exam, for instance, the right way of passing a driving test, and if you are to believe the purists out there the right way to purchase and assemble a loadout for the skirmish field, but that's when budgets and affordability goes out of the window. If KSK is the route you want to go down, and you want to take your loadout to the next level, then you'll need to bring Lindnerhof Taktik into your life.

HL PLATE CARRIER WITH QUICK-RELEASE SYSTEM

Designed as a lightweight one-size-fits-all plate carrier, this model features a quick-release system on the shoulder straps and waist belt. Manufactured from what Lindnerhof describe as a hybrid laminate the platform is extremely tear resistant and will live up to anything a skirmish field will throw at it.

The vest's quick-release system is based on two hook buckles, on both the shoulder straps and torso. Designed so that a real-world operator can ditch their vest in a hurry the system is operated by simply pulling a cord, which is a welcome alternative to the hook-and-loop closure that so many modern vests reply upon. There are more than enough laser-cut MOLLE attachment points to fill your pouch requirements on the front and back of the platform, while a weight-saving MOLLE-compatible skeleton waist belt secures the plate carrier and offers alternative pouch placement for the side armour pockets.

Features:

- Quick-release system
- Hybrid laminate
- Separate compartments for soft and hard armour
- Expandable with side pouches for panels
- Expandable with back padding
- Integrated cable loop on the front
- Made in accordance with the TL standards of the Bundeswehr
- One size fits all
- Weight: 760g   Available from www.hqg.de

HL LOW VIS PLATE CARRIER

Designed as a covert plate carrier, this simple system lends itself to an overt platform that can be worn with a chest rig on the skirmish field. The shoulders and waist are adjustable. The skeleton belt will allow you to attach a minimum amount of MOLLE compatible pouches if you want to. A large hoop and loop panel gives you more than ample patch placement alternatives. Again made from what the manufacturer describes as hybrid laminate, this real-world vest won't let you down on a skirmish field.

Features:

- Designed for concealed wearing
- Integrated plate fixation for hard armour
- Velcro pads for extra length with cover
- Large hook-and-loop ID panel
- Manufactured in accordance with TL technical standards of the Bundeswehr
- Weight: 370g

Available from www.hqg.de

In this situation there is no right or wrong way; there is no set criteria to follow. Who's to say that what you have achieved by spending what you can afford is the wrong way? You please yourself – you're not on parade. If you can afford the perfect gear for a perfect impression then that's great and we would encourage you to do so, but if you can't, but want to resemble a particular look on a skirmish field, that's also great.

The clever players will shop wisely and capture the essence of a loadout, allowing them to have many looks in their gear locker. If your chosen look starts to evolve over time, then that's your choice.

That's precisely what we try to achieve here at *Airsoft International* by pointing you in a direction and throwing affordable products at you. Hopefully, we have pointed you in a direction that you have never thought of before. What you do after that introduction is entirely up to you and the budget you have to spend.

SHOPPING LIST

Flecktarn Helmet Cover
Clawgear Aviceda Fleece Hoody
Combat Shirt
Predator Combat Trousers
Invader Gear Reaper Plate Carrier

Available from Airsoft Zone.com
www.airsoftzone.com

CHAPTER EIGHT

TASK FORCE BLACK

Task Force Black was the name for the UK Special Forces rotation in Iraq during the fight against al-Qaeda in Iraq. By the end of 2005, 22 SAS had been given responsibility for Iraq, with the SBS taking Afghanistan, and Task Force Black became increasingly integrated within, and important to, the US Joint Special Operations Command (JSOC). The SAS was granted full access to American intelligence and targets and took on a pivotal role hitting al-Qaeda targets in Baghdad.

This deployment saw an infusion of American DCU/ACU and good old-fashioned British DMP worn by British forces on the ground in Iraq as the various task forces became increasingly integrated – it's a great look and one that easily translates to the skirmish field.

TASK FORCE 145

Later renamed Task Force 88, this was a Coalition Special Operations Task Force during the Iraq War and comprised several elements of the SAS, the Special Reconnaissance Regiment (SRR), 18 (UKSF) Signal Regiment (18 SR) and US Army Delta who jointly formed Task Force Black. It is also believed that the SBS bolted onto Task Force 145 too, and all were supported by 1 Para now known as the Special Forces Support Group (SFSG), who were identified as Task Force Maroon. Other task forces in the group consisted of Task Force Blue, US Navy SEALs from DEVGRU (Seal Team 6), Task Force Green, Delta and Task Force Orange, made up of the signals and intelligence.

The whole task force thing gets confusing to say the least, but the best way to understand it is to take Task Force 145, now called Task Force 88, as the collective name, or umbrella organization, that all of the other task forces sit underneath. The reason Task Force145 changed its name to Task Force 88 was simply that the tasking of the group changed, and in a similar way Task Force Black changed to Task Force Knight. However, Task Force Maroon kept its designation the same as its role didn't change whether it supported Task Force Black or Task Force Knight.

The really interesting thing here is that only Task Force Black/Knight had all of the trades in one task force – direct action and surveillance from the SAS and SBS (if present), with even a sprinkling of reconnaissance from the SRR, communication from 18 (UKSF) Signal Regiment and support from the SFSG! Now bear with us here. Task Force Blue – you remember them? The Navy SEAL lot – they would have been supported by the Marines (who were not part of a task force); Delta would have been supported by the good old units from the American Regular Army.

The sole purpose of the entire American-led task force was to hunt down senior members of al-Qaeda in Iraq. Task Force Black, operating out of their base called "The Station" within Baghdad's Green Zone, was responsible for tracking down Saddam Hussein's sons (Uday and Qusay) in 2003 to a property in Mosul, but had its thunder stolen when its request to raid the house was denied only to have US Delta and the 101st Airborne attack the building. The raid resulted in the deaths of both Uday and Qusay.

Some two years later Operation *Marlborough* saw snipers from Task Force Black engage and neutralize an insurgent bomb squad before they could reach their targets. In 2006 the SAS was called upon again – this time to rescue British activist Norman Kember and two Canadians who had been kidnapped in Baghdad

SAS assaulters from Task Force Black in Iraq, 2006, wearing American ACU and DCU-pattern uniforms, and Ranger-green Paraclete RAV plate carriers with chest-mounted holsters for their SIG-Sauer P226 pistols. (Leigh Neville)

![up arrow] SAS assaulters from Task Force Black in Iraq, 2006, wearing American ACU and DCU-pattern uniforms, and Ranger-green Paraclete RAV plate carriers with chest-mounted holsters for their SIG-Sauer P226 pistols. (Leigh Neville)

![up arrow] An image of poor quality but considerable historical interest; it shows the then-commander of the American JSOC, LtGen Stanley McChrystal (second right), alongside the then-CO of 22 SAS, accompanying a Task Force Black assault team in Iraq. Of A Sqn's tour in 2007 Gen McChrystal said: 'I know one squadron that in a six-month rotation of 180 days, I think they did 175 operations. That's going out every night into combat. I got to go with them several times. These were not just drive-around patrols, these were combat assaults. Sometimes right in on the objective by air, more often land away and walk in several kilometres so that you could achieve some surprise'. (Leigh Neville)

September 2007 saw a 30-man SAS-led team assault a house that intel had pinpointed as the location of a senior al-Qaeda figure. The mission was seen as a success but sadly cost the life of one of the SAS assaulters. March 2008 saw another fatality from Task Force Black as an SAS trooper was killed during an operation against insurgents in a town in Northern Iraq.

For the duration of Task Force 145, now renamed 88, the British Special Forces rotated the personnel of Task Force Black on a six-month basis. The British element of Task Force 88 ended in 2009 when British forces withdrew from Iraq. Members of Task Force Black were redeployed to Afghanistan.

Task Force Black/Knight's much-publicised operational process in Baghdad was known as find–fix–finish. Working backwards, the 'finish' part was a raid to take down a suspect, 'fix' involved pinpointing a time and place where a target could be taken, and 'find' was the successful discovery of an insurgent/terrorist.

A report in the *Daily Telegraph* heralded Task Force Black/Knight a success and went on to say that "The SAS were responsible for the deaths of thousands of terrorists in the 'secret war' against al-Qaeda in Iraq".

MICH

The Modular Integrated Communications Helmet (MICH) came to prominence in 2001 and was designed as a series of combat helmets intended for troops that sat within the US Army Special Operations Command. It was seen as a replacement for the various non-ballistic bump helmets worn by its operators.

Despite the US armed forces being issued with the PASGT Helmet, Special Forces units ditched them in favour of bump helmets – skate helmets that were much lighter, more comfortable and easier to bolt a whole lot of accessories to. The logic behind the decision to wear what is essentially a plastic helmet was the fact that drilling holes through the Kevlar shell of a PASGT compromised its integrity and ability to be a ballistic helmet, so why not wear a much lighter and more comfortable non-ballistic helmet?

However, there was a massive price to pay for what was really a completely unsatisfactory combat helmet, with soldiers suffering serious head injuries or even dying. The Battle of Mogadishu was sadly a typical example of this, with SFC Shughart and MSGT Gordon reportedly killed by rifle shots to the head. Whilst no ballistic helmet of the day or even now would protect a soldier from a round shot in a CQB environment it inspired the US Army to create a new helmet to better protect Special Forces and to provide the weight and modularity they desired that caused them to ditch the PASGT in the first place.

The MICH was built under the SPEAR program, and offered three different cuts to allow the soldier a choice in protection and weight to suit the mission requirements.

In the real world the MICH varies in weight from 3lb (1.36kg) to just over 3.6 lb (1.63kg). Still weighing more than its plastic counterpart, it was manufactured from an advanced type of Kevlar that was a slight improvement over the PASGT and a massive improvement over the plastic bump helmets. A cushioned pad system was inserted into the helmet to offer a vastly improved level of comfort, whilst the four-point retention system was copied from the plastic bump helmets favoured by Special Forces troops.

There are three different types of MICH – The MICH TC-2000; the MICH TC-2001, the second cut known as the "high cut" version; and the MICH TC-2002 or "gunfighter cut", which features a higher profile around the ears roughly meeting the profile of the skateboard type of helmets previously used.

The Advanced Combat Helmet has now superseded the MICH as the US Army's go-to helmet, but the troops of Task Force Black were most often equipped with the Gentex manufactured MICH 2000.

There are literally hundreds to choose from on the Airsoft market, and each one is as good as the next in terms of build quality, fit and comfort. Just make sure you choose the un-railed version.

Night vision and/or the correct helmet mount is central to this project. Don't even bother looking for a real mount, and you can pretty much forget a replica set of night vision, as they will weigh your helmet down and pretty much render the helmet impossible to use, but we did find a UK-based individual who makes a replica PVS 21 Helmet Mount that screams UK Special Forces.

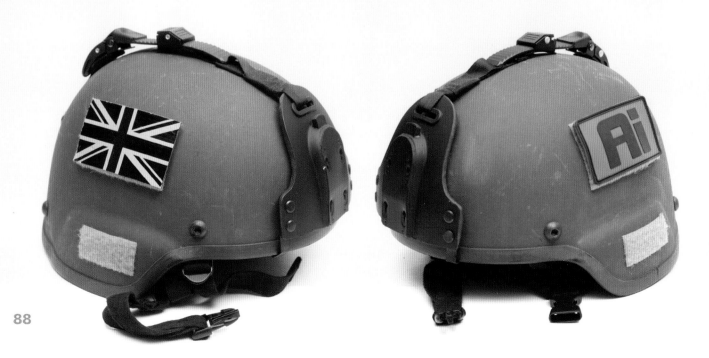

BRITISH COMBAT SOLDIER 95 CLOTHING SYSTEM

It's crazy when you think about it, but DPM in one form or another has been around since the 1940s. The Denison smock was the first garment to sport a form of DPM, which was originally hand painted. The Parachute Regiment and Commandos were the first to be issued the Denison smock, which remained in use right up until the 1970s.

Combat Soldier 95 Clothing System, or "Soldier 95", was the latest and last evolution of DMP for the British military, and was similar in colour to the last revision made in 1966. A four-colour desert DPM had been introduced in the late 1980s and was replaced in the 1990s by a two-colour version, purely because the four-colour uniform had been adopted by Iraq and a few other Middle Eastern countries.

Soldier 95 clothing and equipment was coated with an IRR (infrared reflective) layer which had a reflective wavelength in order to blend in with natural colours in the infra-red spectrum, thus reducing the outlines of soldiers seen through night vision – you've just got to love science at work.

AN INFUSION OF CAMOUFLAGE

A quick online search will show members of Task Force Black appearing for all intents and purposes as American troops, wearing a mixture of DCU/Universal Camouflage Pattern (UCP) and a sprinkling of good old-fashioned DPM – in both woodland and desert variants. In truth you couldn't tell where the American finished and the British started. Other than a few tell-tale signs (we will get to that later), your palette of choice is pretty wide on this one – it's simply a case of the correct era of camouflage that suits your taste – but whatever you choose, you're not going to fall too far from the tree. The one small problem with this project was sourcing the correct kit for a mission that took place some 15 years ago, which has resulted in some items simply not being available, or if they were, the prices were just silly, so we've had to think on our feet and look for a few believable alternatives.

DCU or CCU

The US military's Desert Camouflage Uniform came into service from the mid-1990s and has to be one of our favourite camouflages. Known affectionately as "coffee-stain camouflage" this three-colour or tri-colour uniform was developed to replace the US military's six-colour desert camouflage known as "chocolate-chip camouflage". DCU was the go-to uniform for over 14 years until it was ultimately replaced for a very short period by CCU (Close Combat Uniform), the precursor to the modern ACU (Army Combat Uniform). It gets confusing to say the least! DCU, in both its issued and raid-modified uniforms, was certainly used, as too was CCU, which was essentially issued with raid modification as standard.

Universal Camouflage Pattern

Sometimes mistakenly referred to as ACU, which refers to the cut of the uniform and not the camouflage, this was also worn by Task Force Black members either as complete uniforms or mixed in with either DMP or DCU. This pattern was chosen after a number of laboratory and field tests concluded that it was the best camouflage for the US Army. Despite this pattern being the first digital camouflage issued en masse to the US armed forces, it has had critics as it clearly wasn't the multi-terrain solution that the US Army had asked for. The continued questions over UCP's effectiveness led to its replacement some 10 years later.

American Desert Camouflage Uniform

First issued in the 1990s DCU was in use up until 2010 and in terms of cut there was hardly any difference from the previous Desert Battle Dress Uniform (DBDU). However, the camouflage pattern and colours differed wildly. It's interesting to note that there was a late update to the cut of DCU in late 2004 when the US 25th Infantry Stryker Brigade rolled out sporting the Close Combat Uniform, which was a semi mass-produced raid-modified shirt with shoulder pockets, hook-and-loop fasteners and a redesigned collar along with slanted chest pockets, just before DCU was replaced. It's actually quite difficult to identify whether members of Task Force Black wore modified DCU or CCU. The timeline is certainly right for both, but just to confuse you there is also an ACU three-colour shirt available that was never issued in the real world, but is easy to find in ours. Just make sure you have the shoulder pockets on your three-colour desert shirt if you're using this option. It can be home-modified DCU, CCU or even a manufactured ACU.

Army Combat Uniform

ACU is the latest design of American battlefield clothing and it was issued in 2004. It is well worth mentioning as it was first released with the US Army's Universal Camouflage Pattern (UCP), which is clearly seen on members of Task Force Black.

Universal Camouflage Pattern (UCP) was America's first attempt at issuing a pixelated camouflage, and it consists of tan, gray and green (Desert Sand, Urban Grey and Foliage Green) and is designed to work in desert, woodland, and urban environments. This new pattern certainly has its doubters in the real world and a limited fan base in our world, and has proved to be rubbish in certain environments, but oddly is still worn by some US Army units even though it was phased out by the end of 2019.

PARACLETE RAV

Paraclete started from humble beginnings with their plate carriers being produced in owner Tim D'Annunzio's garage in Fayetteville, North Carolina. Some six years and hundreds of vests later Paraclete Armour was sold to MSA, where the brand still resides today.

From what we are led to believe, the RAVs worn by the members of Task Force Black were supplied by MSA Paraclete and were not pre-MSA versions. However, MSA's RAV has evolved to look nothing like the plate carriers issued to Task Force Black so you really do have to look on the second-hand market where they still command a price anywhere between £300 and £400 – ouch! Bearing in mind we are very conscious of budget we opted for a replica vest that will save you at least £200 if not more when you take into account the pouches you'll need to source, which by the way aren't Paraclete as you would expect, but come from Blackhawk. It's a bit of a balancing act really. The replicas out there are great bits of kit in their own right, and yes, they come fully loaded with pouches, but they are the wrong shade of green – OD instead of "Smoke Green".This brings us onto another point, the Sig holster that was used is also from Blackhawk – a CQC Serpa Holster, which is attached to the vest via an early Cordura-covered MOLLE adaptor, which we could not find anywhere. So, for the sake of not having your pistol in the right place we went with the modern version. The other two important points of interest for the plate carrier come in the form of a CT-5 PTT – fortunately there is a replica out there – and also a VIP Strobe.

CONCLUSION

Put all of this together and you'll achieve a loadout that screams Task Force Black. What we have tried to achieve is the look and feel of the subject matter whist keeping one eye on cost and making it affordable rather than blowing the bank balance and going super authentic. There is certainly no reason why you shouldn't go all the way with this kit and nail it, but it is going to cost you a lot of time and a whole heap of money to get it completely authentic. There will be some kit that you will struggle to find, but when there are easy-to-find alternatives that will look just as good on a skirmish field and cost you in some cases a third of the price, we know where we'd rather be.

SHOPPING LIST

Replica 2000 MICH
Replica PVS 21 Helmet mount
CQC Serpa SIG P226 Holster
Replica Z Tactical CT-5 ptt
Replica VIP Strobe
Replica Flyye RAV
Teesar CCU Ripstop Shirt 3-Colour Desert
Teesar BDU Shirt Ripstop 3-Colour Desert
Teesar BDU Trousers Ripstop 3-Colour Desert
Mil-Com Soldier 95 Combat Trousers DPM Desert
MFH ACU Ripstop Field Jacket ACU Digital
MFH ACU Combat Trousers Ripstop ACU Digital

Available from Military 1st (www.military1st.co.uk),
Just BB Guns (www.justbbguns.co.uk),
other Airsoft retailers and eBay merchants.

Paraclete RAV

THE L119

Okay, so we've covered Task Force Black almost in its entirety – but what about its firepower? Well, if you have any interest in the gear and equipment that modern British Special Forces use, the name "L119" will probably be familiar to you. This is the designation given to the weapon used by the UK Special Forces including the SAS, SBS and in certain situations, the SFSG. So can I get one we hear you cry? Well, sort of... but it's going to take a bit of tweaking to get it right.

FLASH HIDER OR SILENCER

Depending on which variant of the L119 is in use, the flash hider or silencer will be different. In recent times the more commonly seen 10-inch barrelled L119 is generally fitted with a Surefire SF556 suppressor. These are one of the easiest replica parts to come across with versions available from Madbull, some ACM manufacturers and also Perr Mike, a one-man-band operation. If you choose a Madbull or ACM version, you will need to cut down the flash hider to allow the silencer to butt up against the foresight assembly. If you are looking to replicate the longer 16-inch barrelled L119, the flash hider is either a regular birdcage "A2" type or a four-pronged Surefire FH556-216A.

BARREL

The barrel used on the L119 is possibly one of the most characteristic parts. For the shorter version, a 10-inch barrel is used, which can be purchased or cut down from a longer part. The 16-inch barrel used on the longer variant of the gun is achieved in replica format via a full 16-inch barrel or the use of a thread-on barrel extension.

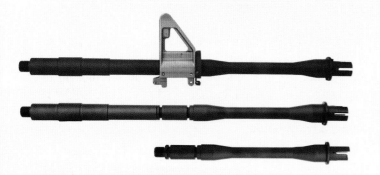

FORESIGHT

10-inch L119s use a regular M4-style figure-four foresight. These generally have no bayonet lug. This is easily replicated by hacksawing off the lug from a commonly sourced replica component. Long L119s use a reinforced figure-four sight that is unique to the gun. These can either be modelled the old-fashioned way by filling the gap in a regular sight with milliput, or alternatively a replica component can be purchased.

RAS

The rail system fitted to the L119 is one of the most common parts that builders get wrong. The correct item is a 7-inch KAC Drop-In RAS of which there are plenty of replicas. These were originally designed to replace the polymer tubular hand guards and mount the gun using the same hardware.

VERT GRIP

The vertical grip issued with the L119 is the KAC Vert Grip that compliments the Drop-In RAS system. Even a genuine real-steel version of this grip is easy to come by and there are a great many replicas on the market from as little as £5.

LOWER RECEIVER

The L119 is built using a Colt Canada C8 CQB and as such it bears its own unique trademarks. Off-the-shelf replicas are thin on the ground, so most decide to have a blank receiver engraved with the exact etchings. www.AirsoftMachineShop.co.uk helped us build ours with their CNC machines.

PISTOL GRIP

The pistol grip is sometimes a source of contention. Generally, the most "kosher" choice is the "Stowaway" grip, sold in replica form as the "Storm" grip. Being a much fatter grip, they are generally very comfortable and the replicas available are accurate to the real thing and good quality. Some users have been seen using Hogue over-moulded grips. If you are building an AEG, this is a nightmare choice, but a gas gun or a PTW platform opens up this option to you.

SIGHTS

In modern times, there are a number of sights in use by the UKSF. The least contentious choice though is the classic Eotech 552. Usefully there are numerous high-quality, accurate replicas of this ubiquitous optic. As such, sourcing one isn't too tough.

For more of a challenge an ACOG can be used, specifically the TA-31 model. This is a little harder to get exactly right as the ones issued to British forces have additional etchings/trademarks. In addition to this, a specific "wing mount" is often used to clamp a Trijicon "Docter Sight" red dot optic on top of the ACOG itself.

Older L119s can often be seen fitted with the Diemaco-style carry handle that is essentially the same thing as the combined carry handle/rear sight for the regular M4, although more rounded off and lightened with additional cut outs.

STOCK

Another characteristic part of the L119 is the stock. The classic choice is the CAR-15 type stock, importantly, NOT the XM style one which lacks some reinforcing ribs. These are available to buy as replica items and real firearms components can be picked up relatively cheaply as it's a simple, basic part. Recently some L119 users have been seen using Magpul CTR stocks. Again, this is a modernization so brace yourself for some chastisement if you decide to go down this route!

BUTT PAD

Typically the CAR-15 type stocks are fitted with a rubber butt pad to absorb recoil shock. The simple style butted pictured is the correct type. They are commonly held on with a single zip tie, a measure we would recommend taking to prevent loss in the field.

ONE STOP SHOP!

Once you have a base gun to work from, the closest place to a one-stop shop for L119 parts is Warlord Tactical, who can be found at: www.facebook.com/warlord.tac. Or look for the L119 Owners Club on Facebook, where 500+ members with a wealth of knowledge are always happy to answer any questions you might have.

CHAPTER NINE

MARSOC

Featuring Ben Dickie

The US Marine Corps Forces Special Operations Command, or MARSOC, is part of the US Special Operations Command (SOCOM) and is trained for direct action, special reconnaissance and foreign defence. The unit has also been known to deploy on counter-terrorism and information operations.

The Marine Corps top brass at the time didn't necessarily agree with the Corps' participation in SOCOM as they believed that their Force Reconnaissance units best served the needs of the US Navy. However, a pilot programme in 2003 saw a unit called Marine Corps Special Operations Command Detachment One (MCSOCOM Det 1) join SOCOM and adopt a roll supporting Navy SEALs. The successful programme ran until 2006 when a command of 2,700 US Navy personnel came together to officially form MARSOC.

However, MARSOC's first deployment under SOCOM command was far from perfect. Afghanistan 2007 saw Fox Company sent home and its commander relieved of duty after a so-called "shooting incident" that reportedly saw as many as 19 civilians killed when Fox Company was ambushed by an insurgent force.

GOING OLD SCHOOL

A quick search on the internet shows MARSOC members dressed in Crye Precision manufactured M81 Woodland G3 Shirts and Pants and not the US Marines' traditional MARPAT, but this is slightly misleading as the original "mission-specific" order was for only 300 sets (increasing to 950) compared with a force of 2,700 Marines assigned to MARSOC. M81 Woodland might be old school but with the Crye Precision twist added it brings this dated camouflage pattern right up to date.

So, why M81 Woodland? Despite a number of different reasons bouncing around at the time of the original order it was a "mission-specific" demand for MARSOC's deployment to western and southern Afghanistan, where amongst other things they trained Afghan Local Police and troops who also wore M81 Woodland uniforms, and as such it was pretty much MARSOC's attempt to blend in with the indigenous personnel.

M81 Woodland was first issued to the American armed forces way back in 1981 (hence the designation of M81— the "M" standing for Military). However, if you dig deep back into the US military's history you'll soon realise that the origins of M81 go back even further to an ERDL (Engineer

March 2013: a bearded MARSOC operator sights along his Block II Mk 18 Mod 0 carbine while providing security in Helmand Province. (Sgt Pete Thibodeau/USMC)

Research & Development Laboratories) pattern that first saw the light of day in 1967; in fact ERDL was issued to US Marines in South Vietnam from 1968.

Woodland is a great look on any skirmish field and with the alternatives we have for you it's easy to get the MARSOC vibe – it's simply down to you – but what we have tried to do is keep everything to an affordable budget. Sadly, try as we might it's extremely difficult and expensive to get your hands on a set of Crye Precision M81 – the prices are simply off the chart crazy.

KEEPING IT REAL

Two things that make MARSOC stand out from the crowd is the Crye M81 Woodland gear and the use of the Marines FSBE (Full Spectrum Battle Equipment), which originally included the Amphibious Assault Vest, Quick-Release (FSBE AAV QR) that was replaced by the Combat Integrated Releasable Armour System (CIRAS), the RRV chest harness, plus a low-profile plate carrier from the FSBE II system that was supplied to the US Marine Corps in 2001.

The whole quick-release system came about from a tragic incident in 1999 when a CH-46E Sea Knight helicopter ditched in the Pacific and several members of 5th Platoon, 1st Force Reconnaissance Company drowned because they could not eject their heavy armour in time to swim away.

NYLON

Most of the nylon gear within the FSBE II system is manufactured by Eagle Industries and generally not on sale to the public. You may get lucky and find the odd bit of FSBE II kit on eBay, but this ultra-rare kit gets snapped up pretty quickly and at crazy prices, which isn't good for this project. For us the fun starts when we can start looking for believable alternatives.

A quick internet search of recent MARSOC deployments shows a few members of MARSOC wearing a whole heap of different nylon gear. So as long as you don't stray too far off into the nylon world who's to say that vest you chose for the skirmish field isn't the right choice?

For this project we went with two very distinct and different vests. The first, and one you'll have to import, is a stunning MBAV (Modular Body Armour Vest); the second is from closer to home (that's if you're reading this in the UK of course) – a Warrior Dynamic Combat System (DCS) vest, which actually isn't that far removed from MARSOC-issued FSBE II plate carriers.

FLASH FORCE INDUSTRIES MBAV (VERSION 2)

In the real world the MBAV is standard issue for many US Special Forces, and MARSOC in particular. The vest can be worn as a standalone ultra-low-profile platform with minimal mag- and comms-carrying capabilities or with a chest rig which is attached via the two ITW buckles provided. The FFI replica is constructed out of 500D Cordura Spandex and has limited MOLLE on the side of the vest to attach the odd pouch. Foam inserts are needed to give this vest its shape and are not included in the package. The vest is adjustable on the shoulders and waist; however, the snug fit of this vest means that larger-sized players will struggle with it.

Features:

- 500D Cordura Spandex
- Limited mag-carrying capabilities
- ITW buckles for chest rig attachment
- Adjustable waist straps
- Adjustable shoulder straps
- One size fits all – not suitable for size XXL

Available from JK Army
https://shop.jkarmy.com

WARRIOR DCS (DYNAMIC COMBAT SYSTEM)

Produced in 1000D Cordura this lightweight, low-profile system is extremely close to an FSBE II plate carrier and was designed for Warrior with direct input from active Special Forces types. Their website goes on to inform us that the DCS is suitable for both Special Forces' requirements and PSD (Personal Security Detachment) operations, but, most importantly for us, it's also ideal for the skirmish field. With gear that's manufactured with the real world in mind, the plate carriers expect to have real plates inserted in them. We're not suggesting that you hump real plates around a skirmish field, but you do have to insert some form of padding, if nothing else, to give the vest its shape and the DCS is no exception to this.

The shoulders are fully adjustable and have an emergency release on one side, which frees the left-hand side shoulder section and allows the operator to remove the rig without having to remove their helmet. The side sections of the DCS are fully adjustable for size and can be adjusted in less than 15 seconds. 3D Spacer Mesh lining is used for comfort and allows body heat to move away from the body's surface while assisting in air flow to provide cooling.

The DCS M4 comes complete with five Warrior Elite Ops M4 Mag Pouches – each pouch holds two 5.56mm mags (including P Mags) – and also includes two Small Utility/Medic Pouches.

The DCS is a great vest from a brand that has been a firm favourite within the Airsoft community. With its close resemblance to MARSOC-issued FSBE II it was the first thing that popped up on our radar when we were in the planning stage of this loadout.

Features:

- Weight: 9.8oz. per square yard
- Tensile strength: warp 621lbs / fill 580lbs
- Tears strength: warp 55.5lbs / fill 51.3lbs
- Abrasion: wear cycles 3,240
- Water repellence: 100 per cent

Tactical www.uktactical.com

ORC INDUSTRIES LEVEL 5 PCU

The first thing that we are going to add to the pile is an ORC Industries PCU level 5 soft shell (spotted on MARSOC on deployment). This lightweight windcheater is ideal for those cold, damp skirmish days and in the real world forms part of a 16-piece, seven-level clothing system which is a go-to item for many US Special Forces operators. At best this is a water-resistant garment, and it did struggle in light rain, buts that's okay as the level 5 was never designed to be a raincoat.

The hood rolls up and stows away and forms a roll top collar that secures to your neck via the full-length frontal zip. There are two large mesh pockets, which can carry equipment, but the mesh suggest that these are more ventilation than cargo ready. As usual each arm gets a bicep pocket with colour-coordinated Velcro.

The PCU used in this project is almost as old as *Airsoft International* (over 12 years) and has been in constant use not only as a skirmish field jacket but as an everyday garment and still looks as fresh as the day it was purchased. Top tip: if your belly is going south this PCU will hide a multitude of sins!

FLASH FORCE INDUSTRY'S M81 GEN3 COMBAT SET

We have already established that the Crye Precision M81 combat clothing is way out of the reach of most Airsofters, but thankfully there are alternatives at a fraction of the price. FFI's M81 Gen 3 Combat Set is a great alternative. Although it might not match up to Crye Precision's exacting quality, it's going to take a keen eye and a knowledge of Crye gear to tell the difference on a skirmish field. The quality and tailoring of the FFI set is pretty impressive and easily sits at the top of our pile of alternatives. This Chinese-manufactured product is one of the best we've seen and for once FFI have produced sizing that's really accurate in terms of overall fit; however, the sleeves seemed overly long to us.

As with a real set of Crye M81 the FFI alternative features a wicking shirt torso, which is produced from 100 per cent polyester and incorporates what FFI call their X series Spandex, whilst the rest of the shirt is produced in Nyco ripstop fabric and features military spec Velcro and a YKK zip.

The trousers are also produced in Nyco ripstop and again feature FFI X series Spandex that can be seen around the knees, lower back and crotch area and do their job not only in wicking away moisture, but also in adding flexibility. Just like their real-world counterparts, FFI's trousers offer the wearer a whole heap of pockets from zip-fastened back pockets to hip, thigh and lower leg ones, not to mention ample-sized cargo pockets.

The trousers also benefit from waist, lower leg and ankle adjustment, but as mentioned before FFI have really nailed the sizing options and make it simple to find a garment that fits and doesn't leave you guessing if you should up or down size to get a perfect fit. At a very affordable price point FFI Gen 3 are a welcome addition to our ready room that you will be able to buy with confidence.

Available from JK Army
https://shop.jkarmy.com

SEMAPO GEAR GEN 3 TYPE (MARSOC) M81 WOODLAND

Raising the bar slightly is this Gen 3 3-D combat set from South Korea-based Semapo, which is even closer to its real world counterpart than the FFI set; however, with all of the care and attention that Semapo have displayed with their example sadly comes an increase in cost and shipping, but that's only one of two drawbacks to what is yet another great combat set that's fit for the skirmish field. The other drawback is the sizing: despite Semapo compressive sizing guide and charts, we found that the XL sample we were supplied with was surprisingly on the smaller size when it came to the shirt, but the trousers were on the larger side –maybe it's just us but a combination of both sizes would have been the perfect fit. The sleeve length of the Semapo set was perfect, whereas the FFI shirt suffered somewhat in an overly long length.

It's produced in what Semapo refer to as a USA Ny/CO (Nylon/Cotton) 50/50 blend, though without ripstop this time – just in case you're wondering, ripstop fabrics use a special reinforcing technique that makes them resistant to tearing and ripping as thick reinforcement threads are woven into the material. That has obvious benefits in the harsh environments of a skirmish field.

The quality is slightly higher than the FFI set, but that's due in part to the smoother finish to the material than FFI's ripstop version, which can be misleading if you're taking the tactile approach to quality.

Semapo's version also features a wicking torso to the shirt and has Spandex inserts in all the right places when it comes to the trousers. It offers the same amount of adjustment and pockets.

It's a tough call: if its budget then the cheaper FFI has to be your choice; if its quality you're looking for then there is hardly any difference, although when it comes down to fit the FFI set is perhaps marginally better. Having said that, we could not decide. Visually they are almost identical, but the ripstop material has got to have its advantages!

We featured both sets because the choice is yours! Whatever set you choose you can be certain they both will easily give you that MARSOC look you are looking for.

Available from Semapo Gear
http://semapogear.com

FINISHING TOUCHES

Helmets and/or baseball caps are often worn, but we've shown you an example of an unencumbered operator; however, there is no difference in the FAST style of helmets you most probably already have in your locker. Comms and ear protection are optional extras that you can do without if necessary, But we went to Z Tactical for their take on ear pro, which again mimics the real-world option, but at a fraction of the real-world cost. They don't only provide you with a comms system but are also designed to protect your ears by blocking out harmful sounds that you may encounter on a skirmish field, and also amplify less harmful sounds through the microphones incorporated into the ear domes.

The fanny or bum pack (dependant on what side of the pond you reside), or if you will a "Tactical Waist Bag", screams MARSOC and is another good option. If you are "all in" like us at this point then the finishing touches take your well-researched and thought-out budget-busting project to another level. The same can be said about the belt we have used. You could easily use a belt you already have in your locker, but if you are following our lead then the perfect choice for this project is an Emerson Modular Rigger's Belt. It was a bit extravagant at an average price of £53.00, especially when the complete FFI combat set is only just over £79, but it's not only a great piece of gear but a great investment that's going to hold the tools of your trade for countless skirmish field encounters to come. We leave you to make personal choices on holster and pouches for your belt rig, but the beauty of embarking on any loadout project is that a lot of the kit we have featured you might already have in your locker. If not, think of it as modular equipment that you can use time and time again in a number of loadouts, but trust us you're not going to move away from the MARSOC vibe for some time to come.

MARSOC Marines fire Mk 11 Mod 2 (aka M110) carbines during an October 2013 advanced sniper course.
(Vance Jacobs/MARSOC)

SHOPPING LIST OPTION 1

FAST helmet
Z Tactical Comtac II
FFI Gen 3 Combat Set
FFI MBAV
Emerson Modular Rigger's Belt

SHOPPING LIST OPTION 2

FAST helmet
Z Tactical Comtac II
Semapo Gear Gen 3 Combat set
Warrior DCS
Emerson Modular Rigger's Belt

OPTIONAL EXTRAS

Orc Industries level 5 PCU
Emdom Recon Waist Bag

CHAPTER TEN

SEAL TEAM 6/DEVGRU

Featuring Dave Porter

SEAL Team 6, or the Naval Special Warfare Development Group (DEVGRU), is one of the most renowned Tier 1 Special Forces units in the world. Immortalized by Hollywood, the unit has also been the subject of a number of television series such as *Six* on the History Channel and *SEAL Team* on CBS.

These shows focus on some of the most famous elements of recent SEAL Team 6 history, and especially the unit's role in Afghanistan where it was at the forefront of the kill and capture campaign that targeted the Taliban bombmakers and mid-level leaders. At the same time SEAL Team 6 was also active in the Horn of Africa, including the famous recapture of the highjacked *Maersk Alabama* under Captain Phillips.

This loadout dates from those years, a time before the advent of Multicam and the ever-prevalent JPCs, a time when AOR1 was the order of the day, and it gives you something that bit different for the skirmish field.

DEVGRU

DEVGRU can trace its history back to the aftermath of Operation *Eagle Claw*, which took place during the Iran hostage crisis in 1979. A task force named Terrorist Action Team (TAT) was formed to formulate and action a plan to free the American hostages held in Iran. The US Navy saw the need for a full-time counter-terrorist unit and appointed Richard Marcinko to head the unit.

The unit's founding members were hand-picked from throughout the UDT/SEAL community, which eventually formed SEAL Team 6 in October 1990 and became the US Navy's premier counter-terrorist unit. The name was chosen to confuse Soviet intelligence

SEAL Team 6 started with 75 operators, and allegedly had an annual ammunition training allowance larger than that of the entire US Marine Corps with virtually unlimited resources at its disposal.

In 1984 a dozen members of SEAL Team 6 would splinter off from the main force to form "Red Cell" (also known as OP-06D), which was a special unit tasked with the mission of testing the security of American military installations. Three years later SEAL Team 6 was dissolved and a new unit named the "Naval Special Warfare Development Group" was formed, but the name SEAL Team 6 lives on as its often used in reference to DEVGRU.

Today the US Department of Defense tightly controls information about DEVGRU and refuses to comment publicly on the highly secretive unit and its activities. It is believed that DEVGRU operators are granted an enormous amount of flexibility and autonomy to wear whatever they want in combat situations, which is excellent for both you on the skirmish field and us. When military uniforms are worn, they lack markings, surnames, or branch names. Civilian hairstyles and facial hair are allowed to enable the members to blend in with different populations and avoid recognition as military personnel.

↘ Skull Body Armour

DEVGRU is formed into colour-coded squadrons:

Red Squadron (Assault)
Gold Squadron (Assault)
Blue Squadron (Assault)
Silver Squadron (Assault)
Black Squadron (Intelligence, Reconnaissance, & Surveillance)
Gray Squadron (Mobility Teams, Transportation/Divers)
Green Team (Selection/Training)

Each assault squadron is divided into three troops, often called assaulters, usually led by a commander (O-5 rank). These individual teams of assaulters are led by senior enlisted SEALs – usually a senior chief petty officer (E-8), but sometimes a chief petty officer (E-7). Each member within a troop will have a specific role.

Each assault squadron also has its own nickname, for example Gold Squadron – Knights, Red Squadron – Indians, Blue Squadron – Pirates. The assault squadrons have a mass of support at their disposal and more often than not call upon other military specialists to deploy with them such as EOD technicians, dog handlers, and communication specialists from the United States Air Force 24th Special Tactics Squadron.

↑ Ops-Core
Helmet

↓ LBT Slick Plate
Carrier

111

WHAT WE DO KNOW

As with other Special Forces' groups, DEVGRU mission parameters are highly classified and open to debate but are thought to include pre-emptive, pro-active counter-terrorist operations, as well as the elimination or recovery of high-value targets (HVTs) from unfriendly nations. DEVGRU is one of a handful of US Special Mission Units authorised to use pre-emptive force against terrorists and their facilities. This wasn't always the case, and back when SEAL Team 6 was first formed its role was purely one of maritime counter-terrorism.

Since the start of the War on Terror, DEVGRU has grown into a worldwide multi-functional special operations unit, which has carried out many successful rescue missions. The current Naval Special Warfare Development Group mission is "to provide centralized management for the test, evaluation, and development of equipment technology and Techniques, Tactics and Procedures for Naval Special Warfare".

DEVGRU also works closely with the US Army's Delta Force and they train and deploy together on counter-terrorism missions, usually as part of a joint special operations task force (JSOTF). The CIA also works closely with DEVGRU and agents from the CIA's highly secretive elite Special Operations Group (SOG) never seem to be that far away from a deployed DEVGRU squadron.

Timeline

The defining features of this loadout are the helmet and plate carrier. The helmet is an EmersonGear FAST Helmet, which takes its looks from a real-world Ops Core helmet placing the timeline anywhere from 2009 until the present day. However, narrowing the timeline is the tactical nylon that we have issued, the LBT Slick plate carrier. We know that Crye's JPC was first seen at SHOT Show in 2010 and we suspect that DEVGRU's love affair with all things Crye followed shortly thereafter, placing this loadout between 2009 and the latter part of 2010. That would also bring AOR1 into play.

EMERSONGEAR FAST HELMET

Emerson produces several styles of helmets, which come in several different thicknesses and weights. The one chosen is the FAST PJ version, which at £33.00 and a weight of 585g is the most expensive in the range. There are, however, only very slight differences across the range. For instance, the FAST MH version is an enclosed helmet, which is slightly heavier and cheaper, but virtually the same helmet. The third helmet in the range – the BJ Helmet – is the lightest and most affordable and is seen as their entry-level helmet.

The most important feature of any helmet is not how it looks or what accessories it comes with but the comfort and protection it offers you. There are two different sizes of internal pads with the PJ version and these attach to the inside of the helmet in predetermined positions, which allows you to somewhat customise the fit, and can be tightened or loosened with the OCC dial and chin strap. It really is a delicate balancing act to get this helmet to fit comfortably, and we found ourselves removing some of the internal pads for the best fit results – though this reduces the helmet's ability to do its job. It's not the perfect situation, but this does depend on the size and shape of your head. All three helmets in the range are lightweight and affordable, and have a comfortable fit.

One point to mention is that this version of the helmet is a representation of a bump helmet and not a simulation of the ballistic version. The easy way to identify what version you want is that the bump helmet will have a ventilated shell, whereas the ballistic version will have a solid shell.

ORC INDUSTRIES LEVEL 5 PCU

During the early stages of the war in Afghanistan, US forces struggled with the extreme differences in temperature, especially the cold weather conditions. As a direct result of poor cold weather issue clothing, the US Army Soldier Systems Center was tasked with finding a solution.

The development of the Protective Combat Uniform (PCU) system was a radical rethinking of a clothing system, which pretty much took its lead from textiles already in use in the civilian mountaineering industry.

The PCU project is a multi-level system which helps protect the soldier from cold and wet weather, ranging from 45 degrees down to -50 degrees, but above all the system is lightweight and highly compressible making any clothing in the system lightweight and easy to stow.

The PCU system is designed to be mission specific, and there is no hard and fast solution to the layers that an individual uses. It can be a bit of trial and error, working out which layers best suit, as everyone's metabolic rates are different, but the beauty of the systems is that you can add and subtract different layers until you find your comfort zone in any weather conditions.

The PCU system of clothing is produced from synthetic materials that don't retain water. While they may become wet, they're designed to dry quickly, which is the perfect solution for any skirmish field the world over.

There are several different layers in a PCU system ranging from underwear through to an outer garment (level 7) which is designed to fit over body armour. However, for this deployment, we have issued a mid-ranged level 5 layer, which is a highly mobile soft-shell jacket featuring tie-downs inside the pockets for stowing gear and a hood. In fact, a testament to the durability of this mid-layer jacket is that it is well over ten years old and has been worn on many skirmish field battles and numerous trips all over the world.

Features:

- One part of a seven-layer system
- Pockets with mesh lining
- Velcro shoulder pockets
- Lightweight and highly compressible
- Durability

AOR1

The AOR1 camouflage pattern (Area of Responsibility – in this case, Desert) is very similar to the MARPAT worn by the US Marine Corps, and is in fact based on an earlier version of MARPAT that was turned down by the Marines.

AOR1, and the woodland variant AOR2, were introduced with the Naval Working Uniform (NWU) Type II, first issued in early 2010. The Type II was only for Naval Special Warfare units which remains the case to this day. In the film and TV depictions of SEALs it is quite common to see a mixture of AOR1 and AOR2, along with the ubiquitous Multicam and, if you look closely enough, a bit of MARPAT given that all important Crye Precision twist. This version of AOR1 has featured previously in *Airsoft International*, and it's a good piece of gear to have in your locker, one that will save you time and money across a number of different loadouts.

This TMC Gen III pair of trousers is manufactured from a durable ripstop polycotton material which is a perfect solution for a harsh skirmish field environment. This man-made fabric is created by using a special reinforcing technique that makes the material resistant to tearing and ripping. Essentially, the weaving process introduces a thick reinforcement thread which is interwoven at regular intervals throughout the material.

The trousers also feature multiple adjuster points to achieve the desired fit. The waist of the trousers is adjustable and elasticised, with a hook-and-loop zip fly. There are more than enough pockets on this garment, echoing its real-world counterpart. The knees and rear of the waistband feature flexible areas, not only to help with fit and comfort but also an essential part of ventilation.

The entire set of this Gen 3 Combat Advanced Combat Uniform is also coated with Teflon, which increases the water resistance of this uniform and also protects against moisture leaving the body.

Many other manufacturers are producing their take on very similar, if not identical, products. All of them have near-identical production values, but the most important things that stand out for us about the TMC range of combat clothing are its availability, affordability and sizing.

Available from Weapon 762
www.weapon762.com

Features:

- Hook-and-loop zip fly
- Elasticated adjustable waist
- Thigh pockets
- Cargo pockets
- Ankle pockets
- Knee retention straps
- Ankle fastener
- ABS removable knee pads
- Re-enforced sear/drawstring bottoms
- Size options up to XXL
  (caution, fitting is on the small side)

8FIELDS SKULL BODY ARMOUR

Styled on a real-world PACA vest, this example portrays the US Navy SEAL's version. This full-torso, low-profile soft armour vest is made from 600D polyester and has been treated with a waterproof finish. A perfect combination to also be worn under the LBT slick, just as it was designed to be worn in the real world.

Built around the soft armour pockets (front and back), the vest is adjustable for height and girth and has more than ample hook-and-loop fastener panels allowing for the placement of any number of patches. Due to the vest's waterproof coating, you will not only be able to stay cool and dry but more importantly comfortable if you choose to wear this vest under a plate carrier or chest rig. For that "high-speed, low-drag" approach ditch your nylon gear in favour of a simple belt order and benefit from the freedom this vest offers you on the skirmish field. In our opinion, this is a must-have addition to your gear locker at a very affordable price. The fake armour inserts are rigid and uncomfortable though (especially in the front pocket) and also a potential risk if you were to fall.

Features:

- Large hook-and-loop panel
- Foam inserts
- Adjustable shoulder strap
- Adjustable waist straps
- 600D polyester (waterproof)
- One size fits all — not suitable for size XXXL

Available from Taiwangun
www.taiwangun.com

LBT 6094

It is no secret that LBT work very closely with the SEAL community in general and DEVGRU in particular, and have collaborated with SEAL operators on a number of projects, including the 6094 Slick plate carrier. The vest can be identified for sizing purposes by the letter A or B following the item number. The Slick can be broken down into four main parts: an elasticized cummerbund, front and rear panels, and an optional MOLLE assault panel. Three versions of the Slick have been released, with the third being around four years old now, and because there are only subtle differences you could possibly get away with any of the three, but keeping with the timeline with this loadout we've issued the first version. The front of the Slick features an admin panel with a Velcro loop square allowing you to fix on a whole array of patches. Directly underneath is a utility pocket that is five inches deep, again with Velcro closure, which you can easily holster a pistol or any number of skirmish field essentials in.

The rear panel features six columns and three rows of MOLLE, as well as loops for the cummerbund, which is elasticized and secures to the front of the rig via Velcro and is held firmly in place with a securing flap.

On its own, the Slick is a low-profile piece of kit that really does need the help of a chest rig, or in this case LBT's assault panel, to bring it to life and allow you to carry those all-important skirmish field essentials. The assault panel has loads of Kangaroo pouches designed to take rifle mag pouches, coms gear and or a pistol; there are also three rows of MOLLE on the panel, which can also be used to mount pouches if required.

- Features two different sizes
- Three different versions
- Optional MOLLE assault panel
- Elasticized cummerbund
- Designed for Navy SEALs

Available from many eBay Merchants

BELT ORDER

We have really stripped the belt order back to the bones with this loadout. The belt itself is a common or garden leather fashion belt which isn't too far away from the SB6 US Navy Seal Cowskin Tactical Belt. To this, we added a duty holster, dump pouch and safety lanyard. It's not going to be to everyone's taste, but we are firm believers in keeping everything "high-speed, low-drag". Of course, if you're going to add more pouches to your belt order, you're going to have to think more along the lines of a battle belt set-up, but as always the choice is yours and yours alone.

CHAPTER ELEVEN

CTSFO 2019

Featuring Tom Rickett

A Counter Terrorist Specialist Firearms Officer (CTSFO) is a police firearms officer that has been trained to the highest level and the role was established by the Metropolitan Police Service in the lead up to the 2012 Summer Olympics held in London. The role of the CTSFO is simply to provide a national capability to respond to terrorist incidents in the UK.

IN THE BEGINNING

Before the 2012 Summer Olympics, the highest authorized firearms officer standard was the Specialist Firearms Officer or (SFO). However, as part of the preparation for the Olympics, the Metropolitan Police Service called in the UK's Special Forces to help train a new breed of firearms officer. For the first time, British Police officers used live rounds during close-quarters combat (CQC) training. They were also instructed in fast-roping from helicopters, which made this elite counter-terrorist unit more effective in responding to terrorist incidents. Other regional police forces firearms officers also received the training and formed the national Combined Response Firearms Teams (CRFT) capability for the London Olympics and Paralympic Games. The police forces received standardised training and also had standardised procedures, weaponry and equipment, allowing each team to work seamlessly with each other should the situation arise and collectively form what is known as the CTSFO Network.

CTSFO 2019

Fancy a break from the usual military look that you'll find on any skirmish field across the globe, but don't want to sacrifice that all important high-speed, low-drag gear? We (that is to say a reader) decided to have a go at putting together a Met Police-inspired look for urban airsoft.

As the end of 2015 drew to close numerous terror attacks and a heightened threat alert meant that the previously shadowy figure of the Metropolitan Police Counter Terrorism Special Firearms Officer (CTSFO) was thrust into the spotlight. Seen in mainstream media, on the streets, in training and deployed to counter threats in the UK capital these elite members of the Metropolitan Armed Police rose to a higher profile than ever before, causing concern amongst many parties. The sight of firearms brandished in public spaces is unusual in most parts of the UK and, despite more and more appearing in the hands of specialist officers since the 9/11 and 7/7 attacks, most members of the public are still not used to them.

This situation isn't helped by some sensationalist mainstream media reports detailing the gear and equipment used by each CTSFO and making out they are some kind of one-man army. To the average onlooker, the sight of ballistic helmets, body armour and assault rifles might seem a tad extreme, but remember that these highly trained firearms officers are there to protect the general public and deal with any major threats.

It's fair to say that UK firearms officers have never really got the coolest kit on the market, especially when compared to the likes of their American counterparts. This, of course, could be argued is a good thing, as it reflects the fact that firearms and tactical teams are required less in the UK than in many places in the world and that the level of violent crime does not dictate a greater presence and level of equipment. Still, it's nice to know that the guys putting their arses on the line for the safety of the general public have the tools and equipment they need to work effectively though; now more than ever, with the constant threat of terrorist actions on the streets.

Somebody at the Met Police procurement office bought into the hype. Instead, of the old-fashioned navy blue or black coveralls you might be used to seeing on firearms officers, they are kicking back in the trendy tactical wolf or storm grey colour scheme. Arc'teryx tipped this for the top for urban operations and who better to make use of its low signature than the CT teams? It fits the bill perfectly.

Many of the images used by the mainstream media show the officers wearing none other than Arc'teryx LEAF kit, including the Talos Pants and Shirts. We can't think of a better urban uniform to kit out the guys that are essentially at the sharp end.

VIPER FAST HELMET

Viper Tactical once again came through with the goods and their Ops-Core-style ballistic helmet fits the bill. The CTSFOs generally seem to wear a larger-cut Nexus ballistic helmet and there are replicas out there. However, getting our hands on one proved tricky and to be honest they are not that comfortable at all. Since we are getting into the spirit of the look and feel being right rather than the exact details being perfect we went for the cheaper and more readily available option. With fully adjustable fitting systems and comfortable hygienic padding this is the perfect fit.

GETTING IT RIGHT

The CT guys have a distinctive look and style so there are a couple of things that are must haves to look the part. Obviously, a grey uniform teamed with a grey vest/body around and a black helmet is a good idea and also the grey neck gaiter seems to be popular. With those points in mind, let's go shopping. Bear in mind we have featured a very accurate impression of a current CTSFO which has taken a lot of time and investment to create the look. Of course, there are going to be more cost-effective options available in today's market.

TALOS ASSAULT SHIRT

We're spoiled for choice when it comes to covering the top half, and really, our primary concern is to get something in grey. The Arc'teryx Talos seems to be the preferred option with the real CTSFO guys, but unless you can find a real bargain out there, this is also the most expensive

The Talos is designed as a fire-retardant, no-drip, no-melt combat shirt to be worn under armour, and is Arc'teryx's take on the common UBACS-style shirt. Cotton/ripstop material makes up the more durable high-wear areas across the sleeves and the body is made from a fast-wicking, lighter-weight jersey material. The shirt is cut athletically and to hip length, meaning if you choose to tuck it in it will stay tucked in no matter how much bending, stretching or reaching you do.

TALOS PANTS

When it comes to trousers, we are no less spoiled for choice from some of our favourite brands and manufacturers. Again, the Arc'teryx Talos Pants are the ones issued to the CT teams, but to get the look, there are more wallet-friendly options out there – just type "grey combat trousers" into any browser and what seems like an endless choice of alternatives will appear

Similar in looks to the Arc'teryx Drac Pants, the Talos versions are made for hot weather and are more breathable, more flexible and lighter in general. Instead of being overbuilt and bulky, Arc'teryx selectively upscale the build in specific areas making for a robust garment with protection and durability right where its required. The characteristic webbing bands over the knees serve as protection in themselves but also, with pads inserted into the internal sacks, prevent the knees from wearing through prematurely.

We understand if you're worried about the price-tag attached to these trousers, and yes, we agree, they are quite expensive when compared to other brands out there, but you do get a lot of bang for your buck, as well as that huge wealth of Arc'teryx's skill and experience in garment design that can be found in every flap, stitch and corner.

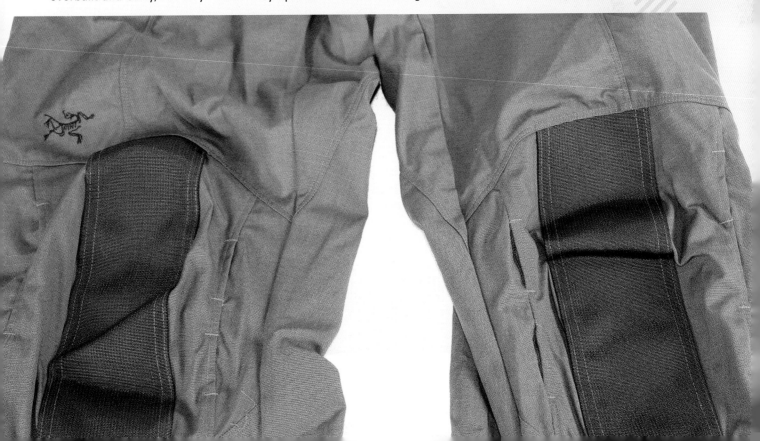

C2R C2ARMOR LITE PLATE CARRIER

Their C2R C2armor Lite Plate Carrier in wolf grey is the ideal choice for this project. It is lightweight and feature packed and very reminiscent of the most popular choice in current plate carrier options. The C2R features more than ample MOLLE along with an adjustable cummerbund and triple internal kangaroo mag pouch. The vest has gone through a recent upgrade with Hypalon laser-cut MOLLE replacing the traditional Cordura MOLLE. There are also new shoulder pads, a new cummerbund and a drag handle system. Still used by CTSFOs today, the vest is also complemented with a groin protector. All plate carriers are basically plate bags or pockets connected together to offer the real-world user front and back ballistic protection. This means that the support from the shoulder straps and closure from the cummerbund are important both from a comfort and a fit point of view.

The cummerbund is relatively thin and flexible allowing you to also take advantage of its MOLLE coverage, but having said that the fewer pouches you place on the cummerbund the better. All we have used in this example are an inverted Fast-Mag pouch, radio pouch and pistol mag pouch. This keeps your side profile down allowing you to move more freely in the confined spaces you'll encounter in a CQB environment.

CHAPTER TWELVE

US ARMY DELTA

Words Connor Monaf
Featuring George Smith

The 1st Special Forces Operational Detachment – Delta (1st SFOD-D), Delta Force or the Combat Applications Group (CAG) needs no introduction, and the unit has featured in the earlier chapters in this book dealing with SCUD hunting in the Gulf War of 1991, as well as Black Hawk Down during the intervention in Somalia in 1993.

This chapter brings the story further up to date as it looks at Delta's kit that was used in the Afghanistan War. Delta deployed to Afghanistan in 2008 following the reduction of US forces in Iraq after the Anbar Awakening. Here they deployed alongside SEAL Team 6 and the Rangers in the fight against the Taliban, and most notably in Paktika Province against the Haqqani Network.

This loadout looks to create the essence of modern Delta while keeping one eye firmly on cost and achieving a unique look for the skirmish field that anyone can achieve.

US ARMY DELTA

As with all Special Forces groups throughout the world, there is a lot of conjecture and speculation on Delta's force numbers, mission capabilities and assets. However, what we do know is the US Army Delta was inspired by our very own SAS and is also believed to be structured in a very similar way.

The *Army Times* staff writer Sean Naylor describes Delta as having around 1,000 soldiers, of which approximately 250 to 300 are trained to conduct direct action and hostage rescue operations. The rest are highly specialised support personnel who are among the very best in their fields.

Sean Naylor further goes into detail of Delta Force's structure in his book *Relentless Strike* (Macmillan: New York, 2015). He describes a few formations in Delta, primarily the operational sabre squadrons:

A Squadron (Assault)
B Squadron (Assault)
C Squadron (Assault)
D Squadron (Assault)
E Squadron (Aviation, formerly known as SEASPRAY
G Squadron (Formerly the Operational Support Troop, grew to squadron size and specialises in advanced force operations, reconnaissance and surveillance and is known to employ women).
Combat Support Squadron (contains WMD experts, EOD, medical personnel, SIGINT and other specialists).

Within each sabre squadron, there are three troops: two assault troops specializing in direct action, and a reconnaissance and surveillance, or recce, troop, for penetrating enemy lines unseen, watching enemy positions, and sniping. Each squadron is commanded by a lieutenant colonel (O-5), and troops are led by majors (O-4). Each troop has multiple teams, each one led by a non-commissioned officer, usually a master sergeant (E-8) or sergeant major (E-9). The rest of these teams are filled out with operators ranging in rank from sergeant (E-5) to master sergeant (E-8).

As you would expect, the American Department of Defence is very tight-lipped about Delta and refuses to comment publicly on the highly secretive unit and its activities. What we do know is that Delta personnel or "operators" are granted an enormous amount of freedom in the way that they present themselves and the clothes they wear – soldiers rarely wear a uniform and usually wear civilian clothing both on and off duty. When military uniforms are worn, they lack markings, surnames or branch names, and are more often than not a mixture of camouflage patterns, which may not be American in origin.

Interestingly the term "operator" was first used by the US Army's Special Forces, which was formed some 10 years before the Navy SEALS and 25 years before Delta's creation, though both of these units now refer to their operational soldiers as "operators".

TIMELINE

Since Delta operators can essentially wear what they like on active duty, this is one loadout you can pretty much go to town with. However, one common mistake is to use the wrong type of tactical gear when you decide which BDUs to wear. Here we have issued our model with a combination of the US Tri-Color Desert Combat Uniform (DCU) and Multicam. We know that Tri-Color was first issued to the US Army in 1991 and phased out in 2006, but the real indicator here is the use of Multicam, which was first seen in 2004 but not actually officially adopted until 2010 when it was first issued to troops deploying to Afghanistan. Drilling down the timeline even further is the style of Crye trousers our operator is wearing. The G3 style of trousers wasn't seen until 2011, some 11 years after Tri-Color was officially withdrawn from service; however, documented open access photography clearly shows Delta in Afghanistan wearing a combination of DCU and Multicam, so we are placing this operator on the ground somewhere between 2011 and early 2012.

TRI-COLOR

The Tri-Color DCU is an American arid-environment camouflage uniform issued to the US Armed Forces. Popularized by iconic movies such as *Black Hawk Down*, *American Sniper* and *Generation Kill*, it's our go-to desert pattern right up to the present day and a firm favourite here at *Airsoft International*.

This desert pattern was first issued in 1989 and was issued throughout the 1990s to the US Army, Marine Corps, Air Force, Navy, Coast Guard and special task force groups. Primarily created for an arid, more open, and less rocky desert battlefield space, it was quickly nicknamed the "coffee stain camouflage" for obvious reasons and was designed to replace the six-colour desert camouflage (DBDU) which we all know as the "chocolate-chip camouflage" uniform.

The DCU camouflage pattern was probably a pivotal catalyst in most players' early days in Airsoft and can still be seen a lot in use today.

KEEPING IT REAL

Delta's love affair with Paraclete is well documented, with the first reported sighting of the gear in late 2001. But all good things must come to an end and Delta have moved away from the iconic Ranger Green gear in favour of the all-encompassing Jumpable Plate Carrier (JPC), something else that dates this loadout. However, the fully blown Releasable Assault Vest (RAV) was pretty much a thing of the past when we caught up with our operator. The much lighter and smaller Hard Plate Carrier (HPC) or even a Paraclete Ranger Assault Carrying Kit (RACK) chest rig worn in conjunction with a CVC soft armour vest was the order of the day, but that's when it starts to get really expensive. The HPC isn't that difficult to get your hands on – a good second-hand version is going to set you back £150, whereas the RACK is going to cost upwards of £400 and if you can find a real CVC that could set you back over £700. There are different replicas of the HPC out there, but they don't do their real-world counterpart any justice and at £150 quid for a real one, allbeit second hand, it's a marginal call. Where you're really going to start stacking up the cost is with the pouches.

Paraclete Pouches:

- M4: £15 each x 4
- Large utility pouch: £19 each
- MBIRT pouch: £50.00
- Twin pistol mag pouch: £15
- Total: £144.00

Whatever way you look at it, you're going to turn a £150 plate carrier into a £300 plus package once you have paid the shipping and import duties from the US. It would be remiss of us at this point not to mention that a company called Toy Soldier based in Hong Kong produce a pretty good and reasonably priced replica of the CVC, but it's been out of stock for some time now. So there is nothing for us to do but become creative in our approach to both the vest and the RACK, which by the way is a simple MOLLE chest rig with a bib. So what we really have is a Ranger Green MOLLE chest rig and a selection of Ranger Green pouches. The body armour we used isn't the correct type by any stretch of the imagination, but it works.

FLYYE SVS BODY ARMOUR

Styled on a real-world PACA this full-torso, low-profile soft armour vest is made from 600D polyester and has been treated with a waterproof finish. It is one of the only examples of this "slick" plate carrier on sale in the UK. Built around the soft armour pockets (front and back) the vest is adjustable for height and girth and has more than ample hook-and-loop fastener panels allowing for the placement of any number of patches. Due to the vest's waterproof coating, you will not only be able to stay cool and dry but more importantly comfortable if you choose to wear this vest under a plate carrier or chest rig. In our opinion, this is a must-have addition to your gear locker at a very affordable price. However, the fake armour inserts are rigid and uncomfortable (especially in the front pocket) and also a potential risk if you were to fall.

Features:

- Large hook-and-loop panel
- Foam inserts
- Adjustable shoulder strap
- Adjustable waist wtraps
- 600D polyester (waterproof)
- One size fits all – not suitable for size XXXL

Available from Airsoft Zone
http://airsoftzone.co.uk

↑ SVS Body Armour

HYBRID CHEST RIG

The chest rig has been disguised somewhat, by simply adding Paraclete pouches to what is basically a Ranger Green MOLLE chest rig. The rig itself is from Mayflower, but a simple internet search will throw up any number of alternative platforms.

The Mayflower chest rig is a bit on the expensive side of things at around £170, but nowhere near as expensive as a Paraclete RACK. With careful pouch placement, you can hide the MOLLE platform with any number of Paraclete pouches and thus make the whole system affordable and believable.

The UW Chest Rig, QD is designed as a general-purpose mid-size platform to be worn with the detachable H-style harness or attached directly to your low-profile armour carrier. The removable H-style harness features loops to route antennas, comms wires and hydration bladder tubing.

Features:

- MOLLE-compatible webbing for additional pouches and accessories
- 500D Cordura ballistic nylon
- Can be attached to the low-profile armour carrier
- Routing loops for bladders and communication gear
- ITW Nexus buckles
  Available from all good tactical gear retailers and a number of US-based eBay merchants

BELT ORDER

Keeping it pretty refined and simple we have used a rigger's belt set-up to which we issued a Safariland holster, Ranger Green pistol mag pouch and a safety lanyard; however, if you wish to keep the gear off your hips your pistol and mag pouches can easily be accommodated in your chest rig.

SHOPPING LIST

TMC DCU Gen 3 Combat Shirt
TMC Multicam Gen 3 Combat Pants
Flyye SVS Body Armour
Mayflower UW Chest Rig
Paraclete pouches used: M4;
   large utility pouch;
   MBIRT pouch

↑ Safariland Holster

CHAPTER THIRTEEN

ALPHA GROUP

Words Connor Monaf
Featuring James Goulding

Alpha Group, or Directorate "A", falls under the control of the Russian FSB Special Purpose Centre and is an elite, stand-alone sub-unit of Russia's Special Forces. It is a dedicated counter-terrorism task force of the Russian Federal Security Service (FSB), which primarily prevents and responds to acts of terrorism on Russian soil, focusing mainly on public transportation and buildings.

The Soviet KGB created Alpha Group in 1974, and little is known about the exact nature of this elite unit. However, it is speculated that the unit is authorized to act under the direct control and sanction of Russia's top political leadership, similar to its sister unit, Directorate "V" (Vympel), which is officially tasked with protecting Russia's strategic installations. It is also believed that Alpha Group can run paramilitary operations and covert operations, both domestically and internationally if required. An important historic mission for Alpha Group was to provide security for the Soviet leadership against enemy Special Forces in times of crisis or war.

Alpha Group was severely downgraded during the dissolution and collapse of the Soviet Union. After the fall of the USSR, both Alpha and its sister group Vympel were transferred to the newly formed Main Guard Directorate (GUO). This relationship did not last long, however, as Alpha Group's command transferred to the Ministry of Internal Affairs (MVD). Another move saw the group under the command of the FSB, finally finding a new home in the newly formed FSB Anti-Terrorist Centre (ATC) where they remain today.

CONTROVERSY

Several highly controversial actions over the years have caused the force to receive severe criticism revolving around the loss of life among hostages.

One of these actions was the use of an unknown chemical agent to help Alpha Group and the Special Rapid Response Unit (SOBR) break the October 2002 Moscow hostage crisis. The FSB chemical attack resulted in the deaths of at least 129 hostages and serious damage to the health of many others, yet was hailed by the group's officers as their "first successful operation for years".

Another controversy was the use of tank main armament, portable flamethrowers, and other weapons such as grenade launchers in Beslan, North Ossetia. On 3 September 2004, the local school was taken over by Chechen-led militants from Ingushetia and was subsequently raided by the heavily armed FSB Special Forces of Alpha and Vympel. The operation was overseen by the head of the Special Purpose Center, General Alexander Tikhonov, who authorized the use of heavy wepaons including tanks, armoured personnel carriers and attack helicopters.

The Beslan siege turned out to be particularly bloody, costing the lives of more than 330 hostages, as well as at least seven Alpha members. According to the government, "the burn impact on the dead hostages' bodies was post mortem", and thus there were no grounds for a criminal case against troops who used flamethrowers during the assault. No ballistic tests were carried out, and prosecutors were not allowed to examine the Special Forces' weapons to determine who exactly killed the hostages, but yet again the mission was hailed as a success by Alpha Group's commanders.

In more recent years it has been rumoured that Alpha Group has conducted operations in Chechnya and Dagestan, while elements have also deployed to the ongoing conflict in Ukraine.

TACTICAL LONGSLEEVE "FLEX" TOP

Everyone knows about the success of Multicam. You only need to look at the real-world military and in every safe zone to see an overwhelming sea of Multicam. However, we were pleased to see that the Russian Special Forces community, and Alpha Group in particular, have their own take on gear. Admittedly the trousers follow the Crye Precision format. However, the shirt is a new and welcome twist on a UBACS called the Tactical Longsleeve "Flex".

Anybody who is familiar with physical activity knows that it's impossible not to sweat, and this figure-hugging shirt is more in line with a base layer than a UBACS. The majority of this shirt is designed to wick away moisture and to provide the best air circulation it can, keeping you dry. The reinforced parts of this shirt include the shoulders and elbows, which are protected by a Multicam layer made up of a material called "Janus". It consists of two types of fabric, which contain special types of nanoparticles or microparticles whose surfaces have two or more distinct physical properties. This unique surface of Janus particles allows two different types of chemistry to occur on the same particle of material.

The shirt is constructed from two different layers. The outer layer consists of cotton with the addition of Lycra for elasticity and durability. The shirt is breathable and flexibile, and basically shapes to your body. The inner layer is made of very thin, but durable polyester net with big net cells that serve as a basis for the outer layer. This layer certainly provides the user with the essential air circulation and moisture-wicking properties that we have all come to expect from a technical garment.

The shirt is extremely comfortable if not figure-hugging and feels like no other UBACS style of shirt we have tested. It certainly has its very own unique appearance and technical qualities and has rapidly become a firm favourite amongst the team.

Features:

- Figure-hugging
- Moisture-wicking
- Lightweight
- Additional reinforced zones at elbows and shoulders for durability
- Size XS–4XL

RUSH COMBAT TROUSERS

Receiving 5-star reviews on Grey Shop's website, these trousers are nothing we haven't seen before. They follow the Crye Precision style of combat trousers and are manufactured from a mix of ripstop 65 per cent polyester and 35 per cent cotton, and are described as a modern combat uniform. They combine such qualities as multitasking, comfort, durability and simplicity. Many types of uniform are developed, but special task forces require the use of special equipment. Regular BDU trousers are not always enough.

"Rush/Natisk" combat trousers take their inspiration from G3 Crye Precision trousers, adapted for the Russian market. The yokes on the trousers are made of stretching fabric that facilitates movement. Also, the location of the knee pads and the fit of the trousers are easy to adjust.

Unlike BDU trousers, combat trousers have much better ventilation, a more comfortable fit, and the ability to install knee pads. The trousers are additionally reinforced in the knees, narrowed to the bottom, and have ten pockets.

Features:

- Ripstop 65 per cent polyester and 35 per cent cotton
- Ten pockets
- Adjustable knees
- Adjustable ankles
- Comfortable fit
- Size S–2XL

BOREAS SOFTSHELL

There is something about Russian tactical gear that makes it stand out from the crowd – a little tweak here and there, a slightly different profile, different textures, and textiles with slight alterations. We've all seen the softshell jacket time and time again either in the safe zone or out in the field, but we haven't seen the Boreas Softshell before.

Single-layer softshells are made with one fabric, but each side is constructed with a different size yarn. The body-facing fabric has the larger yarn, which can wick any moisture away from the heat built up between the inside of the softshell and your base layer of clothing.

Single-layer softshells are by design a lightweight and breathable part of a range of clothing and their main function is as a layering piece, which, combined with different sub-layers, can perform in any condition you'll encounter on a skirmish field anywhere in the world.

The extreme weather conditions throughout the breadth of the country present unique challenges for the Russian military, especially in winter. Low temperatures, frequent rain and strong winds make it important to choose the right equipment and clothes for the given season. A soldier needs to stay dry and warm, and it is vital to have the right combination of breathable layers.

The Tactical Boreas Jacket is made from a softshell membrane fabric for use in bad weather. The jacket has a removable adjustable hood, four front pockets, two inside ones, shoulder pockets with Velcro panels and unique zippers with buckles at the seams for quick access to equipment. The fabric is treated with original DuPont waterproof impregnation; the inner layer is made of knitted mesh, making the Boreas both heat wicking and breathable. The jacket has a minimum of seams and pockets, which provides excellent protection from wind and rain. As for the quality of the jacket, it's a pretty thin softshell, which didn't affect any movement in either a studio or skirmish field setting. The Boreas can be adjusted at the waist to minimize heat loss; the sleeves are also adjustable.

Features:

- Excellent ventilation
- Ergonomic design
- Good protection against wind and rain
- Suitable for a wide range of temperatures
- Moisture-wicking
- 100 per cent polyester, DuPont Teflon impregnation
- Non-porous polyurethane membrane
- 100 per cent polyamide, knitted mesh

KORA KULON ARMOUR

Designed as a Russian Special Forces bullet catcher or bulletproof vest, this simple black replica hugs your torso and screams Russian Special Forces.

Designed in the real world as a lightweight extended-wear item, it is still used by the Ministry of Internal Affairs and different Special Forces groups across Russian today. This replica has a simple foam insert which results in a very light and believable option similar to that used by members of Alpha Group. The shoulder straps are adjustable for height whereas the girth of the vest can be adjusted via the elasticized cummerbund.

TV-101 "NOMAD" CHEST RIG

The Wartech TV-101 "Nomad" is very reminiscent of many chest rigs already on the market, but if you are into your Russian rifles, this is the only one that will securely house your magazine. The Nomad includes four pouches for AK or STANAG mags, two pouches for a pistol magazine, a radio pouch, an administrative pouch and also a removable utility waist pouch or dangler.

The Nomad is what you would expect from a high-speed, low-drag platform – compact and lightweight with enough pouches to keep you in the fight until your next respawn.

Manufactured in 500D Cordura, you know that you're going to get, a rugged chest rig that will withstand even the toughest skirmish field terrains.

Features:

- Holds four AK and two pistol magazines
- Utility pouch
- Admin pouch
- 500D Cordura

TOP FIVE FAST HELMETS

FAST or Future Assault Shell Technology helmets first saw the light of day at the 2008 Shot Show in Las Vegas. The concept owes its creation in part to when Special Forces operators back in the 1990s ditched the then current issue helmets in favour of lightweight (non-ballistic) bump helmets.

These were more comfortable, closer-fitting, and made of plastic making them easier to mount accessories onto, especially night vision devices and communications headsets. However, the lack of ballistic protection from these wholly unsuitable plastic helmets left the wearer open to injury or even death in combat.

Compared to standard combat helmets, the FAST helmet offers a 25 per cent weight reduction. It is also designed to allow the user to bolt on an array of accessories. It's no surprise that the FAST helmet was an instant success and was quickly issued to US Special Forces in 2009

This instant success was replicated on the Airsoft skirmish field and the list below ranks what we believe to be the top five FAST helmet replicas seen on the skirmish field in terms of fit and comfort.

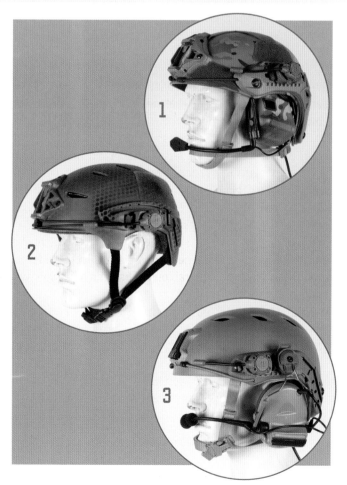

NUMBER 1: TMC Tactical Bump Helmet

Sitting at the top of the pile is this ABS-constructed bump helmet which has an ergonomic profile to better fit your head. This helmet comes with the most padding we have ever seen supplied with a FAST helmet for use on a skirmish field and is by far the most comfortable helmet we have ever used.

The user manual is well presented and detailed and takes you through the placement of the internal padding, which is attached to the inner shell of the helmet via a hook-and-loop system. The padding can be added to or taken away to give you the perfect fit. The shell of the helmet is well balanced, and the chin strap is comfortable and well padded.

The helmet features an NVG mount which is great for real or dummy equipment, but we would suggest that you also invest in a counterweight if you use NVGs as the added weight unbalances the helmet.

A large strip of Velcro runs the length and width of the helmet to secure a helmet cover. The side hook-and-loop will secure a patch, but we can't help but feel it is on the small side. The side rails come with 20mm rails pre-installed, which will give you limited space for accessories.

- Weight: 900g
- Colour options: Black, Green, Coyote, Multi cam

NUMBER 2: EmersonGear EXF Helmet – Navy Seal

This replica is an excepti onal example of what a FAST helmet should look and feel like. It comes with memory foam inserts and a shaped chin strap; the helmet boasts Velcro patches, side rails, NVG mounts and several ventilation holes to aid with airflow. The adhesive hook-and-loop once again holds the comfort pads securely in place to the inner shell of the helmet, but slightly more padding would have elevated this helmet into first place. The side rails come pre-installed and once again give you just enough space to attached essential accessories. There are limited patch positions available through the somewhat sparse Velcro on the outer of the shell.

- **Weight: 500g**
- **Colour options: Black, Green, Coyote, Distressed, Multi cam**

NUMBER 3: FMA FAST Maritime

The only series of helmets in our top five to be offered in three different sizes – small, medium and large – FMA has specially designed this helmet to provide comfort and modularity. The lightweight shell is made of high strength ABS material and features an undercut geometric profile that fits the natural shape of the head, providing exceptional stability and protection. The profile is designed to be compatible with a wide range of existing headsets and communications accessories.

The helmet is additionally equipped with two M-LOK mounting rails, NVG shroud, a set of foam pads for mounting inside the shell of the helmet by self-adhesive Velcro straps, and a fully adjustable helmet retention system. The only reason that this helmet did not place higher in our top five was the comfort level. The fit was perfect; however, there were some issues in comfort across all three sizes, which in some cases saw us having to remove internal padding. The other slight issues for us were the colour availability, which at present is only Ranger Green, and the price tag, which shows that the most expensive helmet in our top five isn't necessarily going to be the most comfortable.

- **Weight: 700g**
- **Colour options: Ranger Green**

NUMBER 4: Viper Tactical Bump Helmet

Weighing in at around 730g this ABS lid is a one-size-fits-almost-all bump helmet following the style of the real-world Ops-Core helmet.

Lightweight, comfortable and well-ventilated, this helmet offers a degree of adjustment via the chin strap and also removal of internal padding. We'd suggest that you try before you buy, as removing the internal padding diminishes the helmet's ability to offer bump protection and comfort from the ridged 200mm liner, which despite providing more than average protection hampers adjusting the sizing. The adjustable cushion pads can easily be moved, which is detailed with the accompanying instructions. There is also the obligatory hook-and-loop strip running across the shell of the helmet which terminates both sides with a more than ample patch display base. The rails are what you would expect and are particularly ridged, which is a good thing.

- **Weight: 730g**
- **Colour options: Black, Green, Coyote, Titanium**

NUMBER 5: EmersonGear FAST PJ Helmet

One in a series of three helmets available from EmersonGear, the PJ sits in the middle of the series in terms of cost. Using the Ops-Core FAST Helmet as its inspiration, the PJ Helmet is the only budget helmet to make its way into our top five. The helmet features a hard polymer shell which is not as comfortable as the higher placed helmets … but it is cheap.

The sides of the helmet are fitted with tracks which will fit the majority of helmet accessories out on the market, or you can insert a number of 20mm rail attachments should the device you are fitting require them.

The side rails also feature removable tab points to secure goggles and masks if needed. Although the manufacturer informs us that the helmet is completely adjustable to fit anyone of any head shape and size, we would have to disagree and suggest that the helmet is best suited to small and medium head shapes. Also, because of the lack of comfort padding we would have to question the validity of it being classed as a bump helmet as there is limited internal protection from the natural bump hazards that you will encounter on a skirmish field.

The external shell features a hook-and-loop bar allowing you to attach lights and patches, while the side rails will give you enough space to once again secure essential accessories.

The chin strap is adjustable and comfortable, but don't go loading this helmet up with too many accessories as it soon becomes uncomfortable and unbalanced.

- **Weight: 500g**
- **Colour options: Black, Green, Coyote, Grey, Distressed, Multi cam**

Airsoft International magazine is the brainchild of publishing partnership **Paul** and **Sharon Monaf** and is the UK's oldest and biggest-selling Airsoft publication – in both paper and digital formats. It has high production values and a circulation that can't be matched both in the UK and across the global market.

The magazine has spawned a thriving Facebook community, which has grown to over 500,000 followers and has become an instant resource for the global Airsoft community. Several years ago the magazine launched its very own Airsoft event, the Ai500, which has seen 500+ players attend unique venues both at home in the UK and overseas in America for a weekend-long Airsoft game.

The magazine is dedicated to thought-provoking reviews of Airsoft rifles and pistols along with skirmish field action and in-depth gear reviews from the UK and beyond.

The magazine has a dedicated and talented editorial team that search the globe for the very latest Airsoft equipment and work closely with the designer and many photographers to deliver up-to-the-minute editorials and commentary from the world of Airsoft.